Poplar Street

A remembrance of growing up

in mid-century Memphis, Tennessee

Michele Adler and

Adrienne Adler Downs

ISBN 0-9766741-1-4
ISBN-13: 9780976674115

Printed in the United States of America

First Edition
First Printing, 2012

Published by
Hidden Water Publishing
Tampa, Florida

Cover photo taken by Lord-Knows-Who, probably in the 1940s.

DEDICATION

To the descendants of

Mary Elizabeth Reedy Adler

(1882-1974)

and

James Christopher Adler

(1880-1963)

WHO's WHO

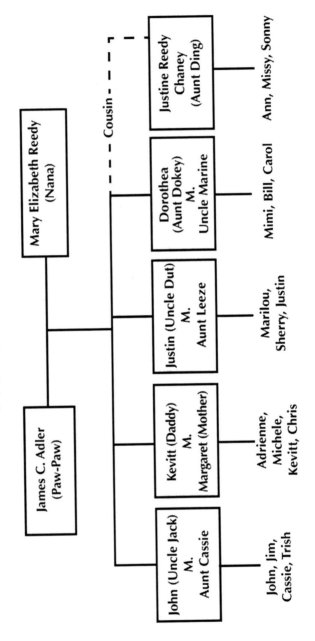

James C. Adler (Paw-Paw)		Mary Elizabeth Reedy (Nana)	

Cousin

John (Uncle Jack) M. Aunt Cassie	Kevitt (Daddy) M. Margaret (Mother)	Justin (Uncle Dut) M. Aunt Leeze	Dorothea (Aunt Dokey) M. Uncle Marine	Justine Reedy Chaney (Aunt Ding)
John, Jim, Cassie, Trish	Adrienne, Michele, Kevitt, Chris	Marilou, Sherry, Justin	Mimi, Bill, Carol	Ann, Missy, Sonny

PREFACE

Sometime during the Christmas holidays of 2008, we were sitting in Adrienne's kitchen and laughing over our many memories of growing up in a three-generational household in Memphis, Tennessee. At some point, it occurred to us that these memories were going to die with us unless we somehow preserved them.

This led to the notion of writing a book. Since it had quickly become apparent that the common denominator for many of our experiences was the house in which we came of age, we decided to name it *Poplar Street*. Within the family, whenever anyone would reference our activities or those of our parents and grandparents, the term "Poplar Street" was always used. Example: "Just heard from Poplar Street about (fill in the blank)".

The house still stands at 1234 Poplar. We should mention from the start that Poplar Street in Memphis is actually an avenue, which runs east/west as any respectable avenue does. But no one in the family ever called it an avenue, so we won't start now. When we say Poplar Street, we are talking about a house, a family, and a state of mind. We're happy to have known all of it.

Poplar Street is richer for the input and the encouragement we received from our family.

We would like to thank our brothers, Kevitt and Chris, for patiently reading the chapters in their pre-publication stages, cheering us on, and relating their own memories.

Thanks go to our cousin, John Adler, for providing wonderful stories of his own as well as some handed down from his parents, our Uncle Jack and Aunt Cassie. Thanks also to John's wife, Jo Ann, for jogging his memory and for transmitting some of his reminiscences to us. And thanks to both for the photograph of Uncle Jack and Aunt Cassie.

We also extend our appreciation to our cousin Jim Adler and to his sons, Chris and Will Adler, for providing us with the Grammy awards story.

To our cousins Mary "Mimi" Rowe Besterczei, Bill Rowe Jr., and Carol Rowe we owe a debt of gratitude for the many stories they shared. Carol is custodian of the scrapbooks and family memorabilia that belonged to her mother, Dorothea Adler Rowe, and was most generous in using these resources to provide us with historical details, which included our grandparents' 50th anniversary picture. We are also grateful to Carol for contacting The Memphis Recovery Center, on whose campus the Poplar Street house now stands.

She acquired additional information that clarified some perceptions we had of the house since the family sold it. We're also thankful to Mimi for her efforts in assembling the Reedy and Adler family trees many years ago, and for keeping them updated. Every family should be so fortunate as to have such terrific "life preservers."

Our cousin, Marilou Adler Mulrooney, kept track of the material that involved herself, her parents, and siblings Sherry Adler Riggins and Dr. Justin Adler. Thanks go to her for that, for her efforts in getting us pictures to include in this book, and for her unfailing support of this endeavor.

Though the book is technically completed, the story itself will always be unfinished. We like to think it will continue throughout the lives of our grandparents' descendants, to whom this book is dedicated.

At the outset of this project, we knew that we wanted to give the generations that follow us a sense of the positive aspects of their heritage, with the hope that they'll be able to look at those who came before them with affection and with a sense of connection.

Every family has its dysfunctional side. Though ours was no exception, we decided to put the focus on the good stuff—the intelligence, the wit, the resourcefulness, the creativity, the tenacity coupled with (a frequently shaky) faith—the qualities that have enabled so many of us to bounce back from some pretty hard body blows that life has thrown us.

What we could not have known in our tentative beginnings was that in the process of recounting our memories, we would be gifted with insights and realizations that we would never have otherwise gleaned. Writing the book has helped us see more clearly that our lives eventually spill into patterns and themes rarely obvious on a day to day basis. It's only when viewed through the kaleidoscope of years that the fragments and pieces come together.

The mystery of family bonds can never be understood, only appreciated. Yet paradoxically we complete this book finally grasping T.S. Eliot's words, that

> *"…the end of our exploring*
> *Is to arrive where we started,*
> *And know the place for the first time."*

Michele Adler
Adrienne Adler Downs
November, 2011

PART ONE

THE CAST OF CHARACTERS

At First Glance

*An introduction to
the Poplar Street house*

Nana and Paw-Paw

*Mary Elizabeth Reedy Adler
and James Christopher Adler*

Mother and Daddy

*Margaret Weber Adler
and James Kevitt Adler*

AT FIRST GLANCE

Every time a truck passed in front of the Poplar Street house, which was often, the foundation shifted a little and then resettled itself. The minor shakes and quivers went largely unnoticed by the house's inhabitants. Slightly more noticeable was the dancing of the foundation caused by the jackhammers used to dig up the street every time a crew needed the practice—or so it seemed.

But Memphis, Tennessee sits on a fault line, the New Madrid, called the New MAD-drid in keeping with the time-honored Southern tradition of taking liberties with pronunciation. And one summer evening in the early 1960s, a mild earthquake did cause the Poplar Street house to rumble with unusual vigor.

The four Adler spawn who lived in the house reacted to the quake in ways that were typical of their personalities.

Adrienne had taken a powder. She was in California on a semester-long break from medical school, working for some pediatricians by day and playing the piano in the less reputable bars at night.

Michele thought it was something supernatural, and kept waiting for a vision.

Kevitt, the only Mensa member in the bunch, correctly determined that it was an earthquake and that the house's side porch was possibly the safest place to be.

Chris slept through it.

Their father, on the other hand, was about to storm outside in a fury, ready to "read the riot act to whoever was wielding that jackhammer at this hour!" He was halted in his tracks by a mighty crash as the chimney caved in, filling the living room with dust, soot and the remnants of old birds' nests.

It would take more than an earthquake to demolish 1234 Poplar. The house had survived three generations of family, Prohibition, and a financial crisis during the Great Depression when a Catholic priest friend of our grandparents saved the day and the house. It had survived an assortment of burglaries, and a small fire or two. It is currently surviving a new incarnation as a detention facility for drug and alcohol offenders that's part of the Memphis Recovery Center. It's reassuring to some of us that at least we'd know where the bathrooms were should we be court-ordered to go back.

Adrienne and others had been given a brief tour of the house at the family reunion in Memphis in 1983. At that time, the sunset side of the house was not yet obscured by the growth of neighboring trees, and it was still possible to see the majestic stained glass window that opened off the mezzanine landing of the front staircase. From the inside, the window remained beautifully intact but the railing across the upstairs hallway that permitted a full view of it had been walled off in the interests of safety.

To the east of the house is an old high school, which had officially been named Memphis Technical High School but was known colloquially as Tech High. Occupying what was originally a private estate, it boasts architectural details which were probably costly at the time it was built and which have long since become unaffordable. During our tenure at Poplar Street, the school's campus was enhanced by many mature trees and surrounded by a brick wall featuring a wrought-iron gate that was always open. It's called Northwest Preparatory Academy now, an alternative school for those who are at least two years behind grade level in other Memphis City Schools.

To the west is William R. Moore, an occupational school fondly remembered because of the sawdust pile in the back, which, as children, we treated like summer snow. Across the street is a Jewish synagogue, which would have been handy, except that we weren't Jewish: To this day, our family consists of the only Adlers anybody knows who are Catholic.

We savor the irony that 1234 Poplar, sandwiched between two schools, was probably the greatest learning institution of all, and resided in good company.

The house took its character from the trees that sheltered it. A huge magnolia tree stood in the back yard, and must have been there for at least 100 years before we were. We remember the cottonwoods shedding their wispy blooms, and gathering acorns and nuts that dropped from the walnut and oak trees.

The knee-deep ivy that once ran amok across the shaded side yard is now gone, and Nana's hydrangeas must have been removed to allow for a fire escape that now drops to the ground from the third floor. No one knows what happened to the sweetheart rose bush. The front yard is denuded of all shrubbery except for the yuccas, and the small stone bench lies upended and crumbling. But outside the surrounding fence with its crown of barbed wire, the sentinel poplar tree still stands, thriving in defiance of all odds.

There had been a time when the front of the house was dominated and partially hidden by a huge evergreen. It had been the family Christmas tree shortly after the Adlers moved to Poplar Street, then planted in the front yard when the holidays were over. By the time of Daddy's death in 1979, its height exceeded the three stories of the house. Daddy had loved that tree; strangely, it died shortly after he did.

Remembering the past is often colored by the rueful knowledge that youth appreciates nothing. It's only when those memories of the past invoke gratitude for all that made us what we are—and what we aren't— that we become drawn to revisiting them. That nostalgia now beckons us irresistibly back to the days when the house was framed with wisteria instead of barbed wire...back to the days when milk bottles were left on front door steps and coal was dumped through basement windows to fire the furnace...

...Back to a time when evergreens grew tall, and didn't die.

NANA AND PAW-PAW

Mary Elizabeth Reedy Adler and James Christopher Adler

"When I am dead, my dearest,
Sing no sad songs for me;
Plant thou no roses at my head,
Nor shady cypress tree:
Be the green grass above me
With showers and dewdrops wet;
And if thou wilt, remember,
And if thou wilt, forget."

-Christina Rosetti, from a poem Paw-Paw asked to be enscribed on his tombstone after his death.

"Mercy!"

Nana, upon hearing what it would cost to engrave the poem on a tombstone in 1963 dollars.

Mary Elizabeth "Maizie" Reedy Adler was Nana, our grandmother. James Christopher Adler was

Paw-Paw, our grandfather. Their union was a result of Paw-Paw's undying love, and Nana's need for someone who could support her in the style to which she wanted to become accustomed.

Everybody's favorite story of Nana's and Paw-Paw's courtship was one that Nana loved to tell. She said that she was being encouraged from all sides to "set her cap" for Jim Adler, and was rebelling.

"That skinny old Jim Adler?" she'd huff at anyone who'd listen. "I don't want anything to do with him!"

At this point in the narrative, one of us would ask, "But how did y'all get together?"

To which Nana would reply, "I found out how much money the Adlers had. They were swimming in it!"

She never explained further nor felt the need to. This was how it was. What she brought to the table, she felt, were her good looks. "I am the body that gave him his children," she said one day when Paw-Paw had irritated her.

They met at St. Patrick's Church in Memphis, which was a popular place for the small Catholic community to worship in the early 1900s. Nana was the daughter of Michael and Anna McKevitt Reedy, and had moved to Memphis in 1902 from Chicago after her father had accepted a position with the Frisco Railroad. Paw-Paw worked for DeSoto Lumber Company, the business founded by his father, John Gottlieb Adler.

Nana and Paw-Paw were polar opposites: She was outgoing and extravagant; he was stoic and practical. She was a spendthrift; he was frugal to a fault.

There's a story about one of their dates that illustrates their differences. They were in downtown Memphis on a cold day, and Nana told Paw-Paw that she wanted some hot chocolate. Paw-Paw said simply: "If you have the hot chocolate, we can't afford the streetcar home."

Nana ignored him and demanded the hot chocolate. She didn't realize until it was time to go home that he was serious about not having the money for the streetcar fare. They walked.

She'd vowed that this was the official end of the relationship. We can only surmise that it was most likely the Adler money that kept her in the game, even if it was unavailable on the day of the hot chocolate caper.

Love and money eventually conquered all. They were married on June 20, 1906, at St. Joachim Church in Effingham, Illinois.

When our cousin Lisa Mulrooney was planning her wedding in 2006, she'd wanted to display family wedding photographs at the reception. It turned out that no one had ever seen one of Nana and Paw-Paw, though there was reportedly one of Nana by herself in her wedding dress. When Lisa modified the search to include ANY picture of the two of them together, it appeared that the only such photograph in existence was the professional one taken at the time of their fiftieth wedding anniversary. In all of the family photos that include them, Nana is at one end of the group and Paw-Paw at the other.

Their yin-yang dynamic persisted throughout their married lives. Nana would spend money with reckless abandon; Paw-Paw would save every last paper clip and rubber band. We never knew him to throw anything away, but periodically Nana would raid one of his hidey-holes and empty it. His desk, however, was sacrosanct, even to Nana.

Nana was loquacious, quick to respond, and never at a loss for words. Paw-Paw was taciturn, as frugal with his words as he was with everything else. The explanation was that he was somewhat "hard of hearing", although this wasn't obvious to us. It may be that he simply tuned out most of the background chatter with which he was continually surrounded lest he be drawn into the inanity of it.

He abhorred waste. When he decided we were using too much toilet paper, he proceeded to instruct us on the proper way to fold a single tissue to get more use out of it. He did not take our amusement well.

Once, when our grandparents were well into their seventies, Adrienne was in the bathroom adjacent to their bedroom and became the inadvertent witness to a heated argument. Nana had just gone out and bought a very expensive new hat, and despite her efforts to conceal this extravagance, Paw-Paw had found out about it. He was practically sputtering with outrage. Nana didn't back down an inch. She told him that he was a mean old tightwad, that he could just shut up, and that furthermore, he could go straight to hell. She then stalked out of the room and went downstairs.

We know that she always intrigued him, despite her occasional abusiveness. Adrienne was with Paw-Paw in Washington, D.C. for John Adler's graduation from Georgetown and his brother Jim's from Gonzaga High School. Their stay coincided with Paw-Paw's wedding anniversary, and Aunt Cassie, Uncle Jack's wife, asked him how it had been, married to Nana all those years.

Paw-Paw laughed. "I'll tell you one thing," he said. "It was never dull."

Nana and Paw-Paw had four children of their own. John William, their first-born, arrived in 1907. His son and namesake, our cousin John, told us that Paw-Paw had been determined to name the baby Johann Gottlieb Adler, after his father. Nana was not pleased. She relayed the information to her brothers, who were aghast that their new nephew might bear such a name— he was half Irish, after all! Whatever might have happened, Johann became its English version, John, and it may not have been a coincidence that John and William were the names of two of Nana's brothers.

In 1909, Nana and Paw-Paw welcomed our father, James Kevitt, into the world. Justin Christopher arrived in 1911, and Dorothea Cecile in 1914. In 1921, two-year-old Justine Reedy, the daughter of Nana's brother Frank Reedy, came to live with the family following the death of her mother.

People were frequently taken aback by the family nicknames, oddball even by Southern standards. Only Uncle Jack, the eldest, somehow managed to retain an accepted version of "John". Daddy was called "Bus," short for "Buster", because of his combative nature. Our uncle, Justin Adler, was called "Dut," because as a child he couldn't pronounce Justin and called himself "Duttin." Our aunt, Dorothea Adler Rowe, was known as Aunt Doke, or Aunt Dokey. For us, Justine was always "Aunt Ding", a teenage nickname that Daddy and Uncle Dut had bestowed on her because of the constant ringing of the doorbell by all the boys who were enamored of her.

Nana had a variety of names. Most people outside the family called her Maizie, a name Kevitt and his wife Diane perpetuated when they named their first dog after her. Paw-Paw used to call her "Mother," or "Dod" which we felt was because it rhymed with "God". She would call him either "Father" or "Gonzy."

The name "Gonzy" originated with a reading text that Uncle Dut had used as a child. It included a story which featured a character called Mr. Gonzalez, whose picture bore a striking resemblance to Paw-Paw. So they started calling Paw-Paw "Mr. Gonzalez," and it was eventually shortened to "Gonzy".

Paw-Paw's sister, Aunt Lizzie, was the only person in the family who called people by their given names, generally drawled out so slowly as to be unrecognizable. When Adrienne's husband, Jim Downs, made the family's acquaintance, he could only marvel at the nicknames. "Ding, Dokey, Dut, Dod," he'd mutter. "Who ARE these people?"

Their first home was a house on Third street near downtown Memphis, where all four of their children were born. Following Aunt Dokey's birth, they moved to 1364 Court, a building they'd purchased which consisted of four large two-bedroom apartments. The family lived in a first floor unit, which was directly above the basement apartment that was designated as a servants' quarters. A silent butler apparatus was used to transport meals from the cook below to the maid above, and thence to the dining room table.

Our grandparents held the Court Street property for many years, during which time its apartments were interim homes to Uncle Dut, Aunt Dokey and their growing families. Nana's youngest brother John, always called Uncle Non, also lived there with his wife Aunt Ruth from the time they moved to Memphis until their deaths.

The building was surrounded by expansive grounds, which would later allow plenty of room for swings, a sand box and lawn sports, and was bordered by a narrow concrete walkway on which we cousins would learn to roller skate. An outbuilding would come to house garage spaces and a workshop set up by Uncle Marine, Aunt Dokey's husband, for his various projects.

The apartment became entirely too small for a family of seven which included three rowdy sons, and Nana and Paw-Paw moved everyone to Poplar Street in the mid-1920's. When the house was originally built, Paw-Paw had supplied the lumber for it and had admired its solid construction. Later, when the owners had to sell, he seized upon the opportunity to buy it.

Nana finally owned a house that, to her, was a mansion.

They endured a lot. They were part of the generation that survived World War I, World War II, the Great Depression, and – not so insignificantly – Poplar Street. They also endured our family of six, as Daddy brought Mother to Poplar Street after they married and never left. We can appreciate now our grandparents' stoicism.

NANA

There are two photographs of Nana in the family archives that together define her. They accurately reflect both the gracious and refined side that she presented to the public and the unabashedly determined side of her that we saw every day.

One is of a young beauty in turn-of-the-century garb, holding a finely-tooled canister of sheet music. Nana had been gifted with a pure, clear mezzo-soprano voice: In looking at this image of her, it's easy to visualize the combined impact of her looks, her talent and her charisma upon an audience.

The other is of Nana and her brother Frank, both dressed in sailors' uniforms and hats that were Navy regulation in the early 1900s. While Frank, being in the Navy, was entitled to wear the uniform, Nana was not. Moreover, it was considered quite daring if not shocking for a woman of that era to wear pants, and the mischievous smile on Nana's face indicates that she was well aware of the taboos she was violating.

The seagoing motif of this latter photograph is apt. Our grandmother was The Unsinkable Molly Brown. No matter how rough the waters became, she simply adjusted her sails accordingly and kept going, where the less indomitable and more practical would have made for port. Like Admiral Farragut's at the Battle of Mobile Bay, her attitude was "Damn the torpedoes and full steam ahead!"

Nana was one of only two daughters born to Michael Reedy and Anna McKevitt Reedy, always known to us as Grandma and Grandpa Reedy, and was the third youngest of their six children.

Michael was originally from New Jersey, but traveled the country in the course of his active career in railroad construction. He likely met his wife on one of these sojourns, though we don't know the exact circumstances. The couple settled in the Chicago area, where Michael worked for the Illinois Central Railroad, and reared their family there before moving to Memphis.

Anna McKevitt was a native of Dundalk, Ireland, and immigrated to the United States in 1870 when she was sixteen years old. She'd financed the journey with the dowries of her older sisters, Catherine and Bridget, who had arrived in the United States earlier and had made their home in California.

Uncle Dut once said that Grandma Anna McKevitt Reedy took a dim view of how he, Daddy and Uncle Jack were being raised. She did not hesitate to share her opinion that the three of them were undisciplined delinquents. Not surprisingly, Uncle Dut, Daddy and Uncle Jack took a dim view of Grandma Reedy.

Once, she was chasing Uncle Dut, intent upon walloping him for some indiscretion or other. He gave her the slip by triumphantly leaping onto a streetcar, and added insult to injury by smugly waving bye-bye at her.

Daddy's only comment about her was that she was a typical Irish mother, who was "hard on the girls, and let the boys do whatever they wanted." It would never have occurred to Grandma Reedy that Nana was simply following her own example in rearing her sons. Anna McKevitt Reedy was not a star in the family firmament, and the chief reminders of her presence in it are her red hair and her family name, both of which tend to crop up among her descendants.

In her defense, she was married to a stereotypical Irishman. Michael Reedy was a charming, exuberant extrovert who had more than a passing acquaintance with the Blarney Stone.

He had the Irish fondness for A Wee Drop, but whether he frequented the pubs because of the dourness at home or whether the dourness at home was because he frequented the pubs is anybody's guess. Like many an Irishwoman before and since her time, Anna grimly accepted her lot, and when she required Michael's presence at home, she'd send Nana out in search of him. Nana, undaunted, would march into whatever bar he currently favored and unceremoniously order him out.

However often Nana had to ride herd on her father, she remained devoted to him. The devotion was mutual, and he'd had a real appreciation of her beauty and talent. When she was all dressed up and ready to go out, he would say, "Go knock 'em dead!" During his final illness in 1927, he told her that he knew she was the only one of his children who really loved him, a reminiscence that always brought Nana to tears.

Nana rarely mentioned her mother, and when she did, referred to her as "Grandma Reedy".

She often spoke of her sister Catherine, called Katie. The oldest of Anna's and Michael's brood, she died of breast cancer in 1935. Aunt Katie had two children, whom we never met despite their being only slightly older than Daddy.

Nana had four brothers. Uncle Frank, like Aunt Katie, also died before we could know him. Uncle Duddy, christened Jeremiah after Michael's father and called "Duddy" for reasons unknown, committed suicide in 1950. Uncle Bill was most like Nana, outgoing and fun-loving; his visits were always happily anticipated. John, "Uncle Non," was the great-uncle we knew best because of his relocation to Memphis.

Nana was always decisive, but her decisions were frequently impulsive while Paw-Paw's were considered. When Daddy was about four years old, he became seriously ill with pneumonia. While Paw-Paw was rocking him, Daddy said he saw a beautiful lady coming down some steps. Paw-Paw told him that the lady was the Blessed Mother. Nana became hysterical, thinking that she'd come to take her son. But the lady told Daddy it wasn't time for him to die, and he recovered shortly afterward.

The doctors had informed Nana that Daddy would never survive another winter in Memphis, where the climate was considered inhospitable to those with respiratory problems. Relying on her father's pull with the railroads and without batting an eyelash, Nana packed up her brood and moved them all to San Diego to stay with some of her mother's kin until Daddy was fully recovered. Meanwhile, Paw-Paw remained in Memphis to attend to the family business.

Not much is known about the extended San Diego visit. Uncle Dut recalled asking one day if he could have chicken for dinner. He was told that he could, but that he'd have to kill the chicken first. The memory didn't seem to be a fond one.

John Adler remembers his father, Uncle Jack, telling a story about Nana conning some young naval aviator into taking her up for a spin in his plane. This would not have been outside the realm of possibility, since their San Diego stay coincided with the birth of the Navy's aviation program there. Pilots were being trained on Curtiss biplanes at a nearby camp run by the manufacturer, and it's conceivable that in those pioneer days of flying the occasional joyride was not considered a mortal sin.

There's no question that Nana would have been game for it. She always had an adventurous spirit, and it wouldn't have taken her long to become bored to tears with both her chicken-killing relatives and her four squabbling children.

If this event did occur, Nana never spoke of it. At some point, they all returned to Memphis and to Paw-Paw—who, in anticipation of Prohibition, had spent the free time engendered by the San Diego interlude learning to distill booze. The family resumed their lives; Daddy appeared to have outgrown his frailties, whatever they were, and grew robust and feisty.

The trip to San Diego was no doubt a result of the panic Nana always felt when children—and grandchildren—were stricken with illness.

One New Year's Eve, Daddy and Mother were out on the town, and Chris, about three years old at the time, was sick. As the evening progressed, his symptoms worsened, and he began making a strange croaking sound. Nana turned the second-floor bathroom into a steam room for Chris, augmenting the effect of the steam with some malodorous compound that she thought had healing properties. She remained with him until he improved to the point where he could sleep.

Mother realized how hard Nana had worked to help Chris, and was touched by her efforts. The next day, Mother took the orchid corsage she'd been wearing the night before and pinned it on Nana's coat. It was a silent tribute from one mother to another.

On another occasion, Michele became delirious as a result of a high fever and was going in and out of hallucinations. During one of her saner moments, she was aware of Nana frantically rubbing her legs with alcohol. Adrienne vividly remembers the scene, and that for some reason Michele was in Nana's room and in Nana's bed while all this was happening.

But when all the family troubles and illnesses were at bay, Nana turned to her favorite pastime. She pioneered shop-til-you-drop consumerism, except that unlike most of today's consumers, she had beautiful taste and an unerring sense of what suited her. The salesladies working high-end retail in Memphis counted on her to boost their commissions, a service she performed regularly. In return, they notified her of the arrivals of new items they knew she'd like, and would hold them for her inspection and probable purchase prior to displaying them.

While she was careful about money in other areas, she had no qualms about spending it on clothes. If finances happened to be a bit tight, she'd just put whatever it was she wanted into the lay-away, so she could pay for it in increments. Using the lay-away was also an effective way to conceal from Paw-Paw the actual amount that she was spending.

Since she was overweight in her later years, she kept her dresses fairly plain, but nobody noticed this once she'd finished accessorizing. She was especially fond of hats, and owned dozens of them. She had a collection of silk scarves that Adrienne frequently borrowed, along with her fine leather handbags, her arresting costume jewelry, and her elegant gloves. After Nana's death, Mother sent Adrienne three pairs of those gloves that Nana's caregivers had somehow missed. Adrienne still wears them.

Leaving the house dressed to the nines, Nana was rarely without a piece from her collection of diamonds that Paw-Paw had given her in the early years of their marriage, perhaps to make up for the hot chocolate business. Ironically, the diamonds would finally be sold to pay for her care after she became incapacitated.

Nana placed a high priority on appearances, and delighted in having others think that she was younger than she actually was. She even went so far as to lie about her age on Aunt Dokey's birth certificate, claiming in 1914 that she was twenty-two when she was actually thirty-one. Nana could have justified the fib because the certificate asked for the mother's age on her last birthday, not the mother's date of birth, and she could have just decided that the last birthday she celebrated was her twenty-second. She was apparently unconcerned that anybody doing the math would have concluded that she gave birth to Uncle Jack at fifteen, and equally unconcerned over possible official scrutiny of the document. We're sure that if necessary she would have been happy to go to jail just as long as the other inmates thought she was twenty-two.

Nana's emphasis on appearances didn't stop with her own. If she saw us going out to face the world without being presentable by her standards, she'd call us on it.

"Hmmph!" she'd snort disdainfully, eyeing the offender up and down. "D'you want people to see you looking like Miss Devil?"

Since we most certainly did NOT want to look like Miss Devil, we'd hasten to make the necessary repairs.

Michele had gone shopping one day and returned home with an impressive collection of new clothes that she'd bought. Mother, as always, was horrified by the extravagance. Michele shrugged. "There's a little Nana in all of us," she said. "Some more than others."

To this day, it's rare that either of us will appear in public without donning Full Battle Regalia: hair in place, makeup perfect, and—to use Nana's words— "dressed fit to kill".

During the Kennedy Administration when Camelot was in full flower, Uncle Jack and Aunt Cassie invited Nana to Washington to accompany them to a party held at Hickory Hill, the home of Bobby and Ethel Kennedy. Bobby was the Attorney General at the time, and Uncle Jack, as head of the Administrative Division at the Department of Justice, reported to him and was included on the guest list for the event.

The evening was a highlight of Nana's life. Upon meeting her, Bobby said, "I see where Jack gets his good looks!" In addition, Nana somehow won the trust of the Kennedy dog, which saw her, sat down beside her, and remained next to her for the duration of the party. Even Ethel Kennedy commented that it was very much unlike the dog to take to anyone outside of the family.

Nana was not known for her driving skills. Our cousin Mimi Rowe Besterczei, Aunt Dokey's eldest daughter, reminded us of the story about Nana's initial experience behind the wheel. When the first automobiles came on the market, she was determined to take one out for a spin. The details are vague about whose car it was and how she managed to cajole the owner into letting her anywhere near it, but—as usual—she got her way. Off she went, and things proceeded uneventfully until she realized she had a problem: She had no idea how to stop. She kept driving round and round the block, screaming for help every time she passed the cluster of people gathered to watch, until she finally ran out of gas. We presume she somehow avoided both scaring the horses in the street and colliding with any of them.

When we were in our teens, Nana drove a 1948 Dodge that she'd bought from Daddy. It looked like a baby-blue Sherman tank without the treads, and its solid steel chassis was almost as indestructible. The car featured something called Fluid Drive, which allowed the car to be driven like one with automatic transmission, but still retained the clutch. Kevitt said that based upon his experience with it, he thought he knew how to drive a real manual transmission. He was proven totally wrong in the summer of 1965 when John Adler came to town and let Kevitt drive his new GTO. He stalled it repeatedly thanks to his Fluid Drive training.

Needless to say, Nana never did get the hang of it.

One afternoon during rush hour, she was stopped at a light on Union Avenue on her way home from one of her shopping expeditions. She was on an incline, trying to keep the brake and the clutch working in sync, and failing miserably. She'd put on the brake, then let it off while she hit the clutch, causing the car to roll backwards and strike the one behind her. Then she'd give it enough gas to roll it forward, and the process would start all over again. After the third time this happened, the owner of the car she'd kept assaulting got out, came up to her open window and proceeded to lambaste her.

So she sued him, claiming a whiplash injury.

And won $1500.

"Well!" she sniffed. "I'd have let it go if he hadn't been so TACKY about it!"

The sight of the blue tank towering over all the other vehicles and making its haphazard approach down the street struck fear into the hearts of those witnessing it. Nana made her turns hand over hand, an inch at a time, and was slow pulling into traffic. Mimi, who lived to bear witness to a number of perilous events involving our grandmother and her car, tells of an incident shortly before Nana's driving privileges were permanently revoked. Nana was making a left turn from our side street onto busy Poplar. She was taking her usual time about it, but apparently had not noticed a bus that was bearing down on them. Mimi, not wanting to frighten Nana into doing something REALLY stupid, kept quiet. As Mimi watched the bus coming, thinking detachedly that either they were going to die or they weren't, it slowed and stopped. Nana had cheated death again. Mimi didn't tell her mother about what had happened until Nana was safely grounded.

The car keys were retired for good following a report from one of Aunt Dokey's neighbors that Nana had been spotted in her car on Union Avenue, driving along while straddling the yellow line. Mimi thought that Nana appeared relieved that she wouldn't have to drive any more.

Daddy eventually sold the car to two hippies who stopped at Poplar Street during the estate sale after Nana's death. The hippies were mightily impressed with Nana's hat collection, and bought a hat "to go with the car."

Nana never feared a confrontation. Either her charm or her sheer bravado would always save the day.

One afternoon, a couple had been engaging in amorous activity near the sawdust pile behind the technical school next door. Apparently things were getting out of hand, and the woman began screaming.

The racket alerted Nana, who ran out onto the balcony off our parents' bedroom in time to hear the woman cry "Stop! You're ruining my life!" Raising her trained voice to its full power, Nana began shouting at the two of them. There was an abrupt silence, and presumably the mood was broken. With Nana manning the ramparts, we're fully confident that the sawdust tryst was never consummated.

This was not her first balcony scene. Uncle Dut told of one that took place after he and Daddy had been out partying in their youth, and had come home very late. Daddy was pretty drunk, and refused to get out of the car. The more Uncle Dut tried to coax him into the house, the more belligerent Daddy became. Finally, Uncle Dut just left him there, not wanting to risk a bloody nose for a good deed. Daddy remained in the car and, to put it euphemistically, slept.

Nana, who'd heard only one set of footsteps come in when two had gone out hours earlier, stepped once more unto the breach and onto the balcony.

At maximum throttle, she yelled, "KEVITT ADLER, GET IN THIS HOUSE THIS MINUTE!"

Daddy emerged from the car immediately, and walked a perfectly straight line into the house. He had literally willed himself sober. Nana was that effective.

Michele was talking with Daddy one time, discussing with him a problem she was having. She told him, "This is an occasion where one has to ask, 'What would Nana do?'" He laughed, and responded, "She always said to be there the firstest with the mostest!"

She usually was.

When we asked ourselves what Nana would do, the answers were usually much more practical than those solicited when asking What Jesus Would Do. Jesus, for example, would probably not have advocated mopping the floor with the car salesman who was trying to swindle Adrienne when she bought her son Mark's truck shortly after her husband's death. Adrienne simply pretended she was Nana and got the deal she wanted.

Nana started to decline noticeably after Paw-Paw's death in 1963.

By 1964, she was becoming visibly confused. She talked incessantly through the weddings of our cousins, Marilou Adler Mulrooney and Sherry Adler Riggins, in 1964 and 1967.

One morning when Adrienne and Jim Downs were visiting Memphis shortly before their marriage in 1966, Jim was shaving in the bathroom adjacent to Nana's bedroom. She barged in on him, convinced he was Uncle Dut, and refused to believe he was anyone else. Jim finally escaped, shaken. Later, she gave Adrienne a silver dish for a wedding present, not realizing it belonged to our mother.

She developed dementia at a time when Alzheimer's was thought to be a disease of younger people, so her lapses were attributed to senility. It was difficult to spot the early signs, because she'd tried hard to cover them up.

Adrienne discovered the extent of Nana's success in hiding her symptoms the time she drove to Memphis in 1971 and let herself into Poplar Street unannounced. Mother wasn't there, and Nana, who by then was deep in the throes of her disease, thought that the noise she heard downstairs was Mother.

Nana began calling, "Margaret? Margaret, is that you?"

Adrienne went upstairs, saying, "No, it's not Margaret, it's Adrienne."

"Oh! Adrienne! It's SO lovely to see you!" Adrienne realized from the bewildered look in Nana's eyes that she didn't know her from Adam.

"I've heard SO many nice things about you!" Nana trilled.

Adrienne tried again. "Nana, I'm Adrienne, Kev's daughter".

"Yeess! Kev! He's such a FINE man!"

It suddenly dawned on Adrienne that she'd seen Nana employ this same line of patter for years when meeting someone for the first time, and that furthermore it was her substantial repertoire of stock responses to situations that allowed her to disguise her illness for as long as she did.

Gradually, she started forgetting who the rest of us were. One day she saw Chris and decided he was some attractive man who had come to call.

"I like brown-eyed men!" she said enthusiastically.

Chris played along. "Brown-eyed *handsome* men," he corrected, channeling his inner Chuck Berry for the occasion.

Living at Poplar Street while attending college, Chris had become adept at humoring Nana's deluded notions. One evening Nana became quite agitated, convinced that she'd be late for choir practice and that Mr. Hayes, the director, would be upset. Mr. Hayes, of course, was long dead, and she hadn't attended choir practice in thirty years.

Chris didn't miss a beat: "Oh! I forgot to tell you! Mr. Hayes called and said that practice was canceled tonight." The answer calmed her down.

Most of her great-grandchildren old enough to remember her might recall a frightening figure.

She spent the last years of her life talking to the personages on her television screen and to the pictures of her family hanging on the wall. It was not easy to find people to care for her, as she was difficult, demanding, and dismissive of the help she received from them. We may as well have had a revolving door though which the caregivers came and went, with more than a few avenging themselves by taking with them whatever of her possessions they could steal.

Mother would dutifully prepare meals for her and take them up to her room. One day, one of Nana's few remaining circuits got tangled. She associated Mother with Daddy, but she also associated Mother with cooking. She became frantic.

"Kev's going to marry the cook!"

She lurched through the upstairs rooms, hysterical. She never did calm down. She just ran out of steam.

In 1974, she died of a stroke the week Daddy was hospitalized for pancreatitis. However demented she may have been, we thought she knew on some level that he was seriously ill. Her indomitable spirit lost in the ruins of her mind and her body, she'd finally been given more than she could handle. A nurse who was with her when she died said that Nana opened her mouth and emitted a sound that was exactly like that of a harp.

Her death was a relief. In a final bit of irony, Daddy was too sick to attend her funeral. It was left to the rest of us to bury her in Calvary Cemetery in the hot July sun, just as we had buried Paw-Paw and just as we would bury Mother and Daddy.

Always, it seems, they'd leave in summer.

PAW-PAW

Paw-Paw was 6 foot 2 and weighed perhaps 140 pounds, a physique that inspired Nana's derisive "skinny Jim Adler" comment. He was one of those men whose looks improve as they mature. He had a shock of beautiful white hair that, even in his old age, people would notice and compliment.

He was very well-read, and put a lot of stock in scholarship. In Poplar Street's living room loomed a huge ornate bookcase which housed, among other works,

Paw-Paw's collection of the Harvard Classics: Victor Hugo, Charles Dickens, Mark Twain, Washington Irving and many others were represented. He'd once said that anyone who'd read all of them could consider himself an educated man. Paw-Paw knew them in depth.

Nana sometimes griped that he bought books when they were short of money—no doubt leaving less for her to spend on clothes.

A few years ago, our cousin John Adler asked if we knew whether Nana or Paw-Paw had received a formal education. We realized that the only aspect of their schooling that we ever remembered hearing them discuss was Nana's extensive musical training. It's probable that Paw-Paw had some degree of education, given his family's comfortable circumstances and his own literary bent. One theory is that he cut his academic career short to work in the family lumber mill. Since Paw-Paw's brother Uncle Will was a journalist, we're hazarding a guess that the lion's share of the tuition dollars went to him, with the idea that Paw-Paw would inherit the lumber business upon his father's death.

Paw-Paw could add up columns of figures in his head, without resorting to the technique of doing it one column at a time.

Once, at dinner time, Mother made a comment that "genius was 90 percent effort." Paw-Paw added: "Don't ever discount that other 10 percent."

There was a very reassuring solidity about him. He was honest, he was honorable and he was steadfast. His German ability to keep his head when all about him were losing theirs was evident when there were accidents. "Anybody hurt?" he would ask. If nobody was, Paw-Paw would let it go. This attitude toward unforeseen mishaps was one that Daddy shared, and it endeared both men to us.

When Daddy and his brothers were in boarding school, Paw-Paw would write to them frequently. His letters were usually signed, "As ever, Pop." But when he wanted to scold them for something, he signed them, "Your Father." Daddy later told Paw-Paw that they always checked the signature before they read the letters. It was typical of him and his deliberative ways that he'd write stern letters where other fathers might have visited the school and confronted their sons in a more outspoken and physically threatening manner.

Our earliest memories of Paw-Paw were of being bounced on his knee while he chanted a nursery rhyme supposedly attributed to Queen Elizabeth I of England:

> "Ride a cock horse to Banbury Cross,
> To see a fine lady upon a white horse,
> Rings on her fingers and bells on her toes,
> She will have music wherever she goes."

At the end, he'd lift us up into the air and cry, "Wheee!", always Michele's favorite part.

He and Kevitt had a close relationship. One day
when Kevitt was about five years old, they were reading a book and came across a picture of a large bird.
Paw-Paw couldn't immediately identify it, but Kevitt
informed him that it was a whooping crane. Paw-Paw
loved to tell that story.

He taught all of us how to play chess, but only
Kevitt had much interest in it. We can still see Kevitt
and Paw-Paw at the dining room table on Poplar Street,
engaged in a chess match. Kevitt later taught his son
Kev to play, and Kev was part of several championship
chess teams while he was still in grammar school.

Thanks to Paw-Paw, Aunt Dokey's son Bill Rowe
was the first member of his second-grade class at
Sacred Heart to serve as an altar boy. This was because
he was the first second-grader to learn all of the Latin
responses, and this, in turn, was because Paw-Paw had
patiently coached him during one of the long walks
with the grandchildren that had become a holiday ritual. The longest and most difficult of the prayers was
the Suscipiat, the one that today begins with "May the
Lord accept this sacrifice…" On that walk, Paw-Paw
had brought with him his Missal, the book of Mass
prayers. He kept Bill at his side while the rest of us
ran ahead, and kept listening while Bill practiced the
prayer until he had it memorized cold.

Paw-Paw developed a genuine fondness for one
of Adrienne's first boyfriends, someone we shall call
Joe. The two would engage in frequent conversations,
both when Paw-Paw answered Joe's phone calls to

Adrienne and when Joe came to see her. When the two broke up, Paw-Paw was very disappointed. Whenever he picked up the phone to hear a male voice on the other end asking for Adrienne, Paw-Paw would say, "Joe? Joe, is that you?" He persisted for years in comparing all other boyfriends unfavorably to Joe. Fortunately, he didn't live to learn of Joe's later arrest for "moral turpitude", as it was phrased at the time.

Our brother Chris was named after Paw-Paw, and it's a puzzle as to why none of his sons bore his full name. Paw-Paw had a diamond stud that had been made from one of his mother's earrings, and that he always wore on special occasions. He always said he would leave the stud to the grandchild named after him, so it went to Chris, who had it made into an engagement ring when he married Susan Morris. The other stud had gone to his brother, Uncle Will.

Paw-Paw was born into a family that contributed to the post-Civil War expansion of Memphis. John Gottlieb Adler, Paw-Paw's father, was a native of Germany and a Lutheran who supposedly converted to Catholicism to marry our great-grandmother, Eliza Warnock. We don't know how he wound up in Memphis, but his establishment of the DeSoto Lumber Company there was fortuitous in that Memphis was experiencing a period of rapid growth in the latter part of the 19th century. However, Great-Grandpa Adler, for all of his business expertise, didn't anticipate that the property he would later sell for the proverbial string of beads would become part of downtown Memphis.

The lumber and millwork company prospered, and gradually developed a niche market in church pews. As the city spread eastward, a new Catholic parish was needed in the Crosstown area. Desoto provided the pews for the church, to be called Sacred Heart Church. Nana and Paw-Paw would become lifelong parishioners there.

Paw-Paw had two brothers and two sisters. One of his brothers, Joseph, died in infancy. The other was Will, who'd been an Editorial Page Editor for Memphis's morning newspaper, The Commercial Appeal.

Uncle Will died when Adrienne was a toddler. Several years before his death he'd had a stroke, which left him in need of considerable physical assistance. Daddy once accompanied him on an extended trip. His efforts to help Uncle Will during that time left him with a chronic shoulder bursitis which plagued him on and off for most of his life.

Uncle Will never married, nor did his sister Elizabeth Augusta, called "Lizzie". Aunt Lizzie had a highly affected way of speaking, very slow and somewhat unctuous. Uncle Dut could mimic it to perfection, so Aunt Lizzie's voice lingered long after her death.

The other sister, Marie, was called Mair-ree in a distorted version of the French pronunciation. She had two daughters, Elizabeth Bumpus McKee and Eugenie Bumpus Raynor.

Paw-Paw had done well enough to send three sons to a Jesuit boarding school. But our great-grandfather died without a will in 1922, and the business had to be divided among Paw-Paw, his brother Will, and his two sisters. Paw-Paw said there had been an understanding that the business would be his, but his siblings, either unaware of such an agreement or unwilling to acknowledge it, stood their ground.

Paw-Paw decided to buy them out, and the burden of that plus the losses he suffered during the Depression nearly bankrupted him. The lumber company closed. Nana and Paw-Paw almost lost Poplar Street, and were saved only by a cash advance from a Catholic priest and family friend, who earned acknowledgment and a bequest in Paw-Paw's will.

The rift between Paw-Paw and his sisters never healed. Paw-Paw never spoke to Lizzie or Marie again, though he was so discreet about it that we were adults before we discovered that this was the case. Perhaps as children we sensed it, as did our cousins, though it was never discussed in front of us. When Aunt Lizzie or Aunt Marie came around, Paw-Paw would disappear so unobtrusively that we never noticed.

Daddy said that Paw-Paw was close-mouthed about the rift even at its most acrimonious. He said, "When we were out with Paw-Paw and saw his relatives on the street, we'd cross over to the other side. We were never sure why."

By the time the grandchildren came along, we believe that an understanding must have been reached that Paw-Paw's decision to estrange himself from his sisters in perpetuity didn't require the rest of the family to follow suit. We recall contact with Aunt Lizzie and Aunt Marie from early ages, both at their home and at Poplar Street. They were included in all the weddings, funerals and christenings, and were always treated courteously on these occasions.

Lizzie and Marie lived with their brother Will in a dark, forbidding old place at McNeil and Poplar, long since replaced with a small office building. We think that this is also where Paw-Paw lived before he and Nana married. The memory of it still conjures up frightening images. Even John Adler, no more likely to be taken alive as a child than as an adult, admits to getting a case of the creeps once inside it. "I wasn't a scaredy-cat kid," John said recently. "But I always hid behind the grown-ups if I ever had to go there."

The entrance hall was dominated by a huge portrait of Great-Grandpa Adler. As painted, he resembled an unpleasant version of the tycoon depicted on the Monopoly game cards, glowering down on us in disapproval.

The décor of the house represented the worst of Victorian era excess with its emphasis on oversized, ostentatiously carved furniture heavily embellished with gargoyles. There was almost no color to enliven the murky depths of the place, unless one considered the faded Oriental rugs which, to our knowledge, were never cleaned.

Aunt Lizzie owned a series of large, vicious-looking dogs, and she was dedicated to their well-being. When one of them would bite her, she'd proudly display the bandages which covered the bloody evidence. Their fearsome barks and growls gave notice that given the chance, they'd eat us.

For a time, we'd enjoyed the one feature of the house that actually held some interest for us. It was the bell used to summon the servants, who were long gone by the time we were born. It was on the floor of the library, and a small lump under the rug indicated its whereabouts. We'd step on the bell, producing its loud ring, and shiver excitedly as the dogs would go into a frenzy of barking. It didn't take long for Aunt Lizzie to start penning the dogs up in the library on our rare visits, which effectively curtailed that entertainment. Whenever Michele read tales of Cerberus, the dog that guarded the gates of hell in mythology, she always thought of the dogs at Aunt Lizzie's.

Our grandfather prayed constantly, possibly because he'd figured out that he couldn't pray and plot his sisters' demises at the same time. He must have said several rosaries a day, and it was common to see him kneeling at the sofa, his head bowed low over the cushions. Carol Rowe, Aunt Dokey's youngest daughter, remembers him constantly fingering his rosary beads, even as he paced the hospital corridors the night before the throat cancer surgery that would leave him mute.

Once, when they were trying to rent one of the Court Street apartments, Nana said, "With all the praying you do, why don't you pray that we rent one of these apartments?"

Paw-Paw said tersely, "I don't pray for material things."

"Well, I do!" Nana retorted. It didn't appear to change his mind.

When we accompanied our grandparents to church on Sundays, we always sat in the pew which John Gottlieb had donated. The rest of the parishioners knew it was ours, and also knew that Paw-Paw would chase away any unwary interlopers. It was impressed upon us at an early age that the marble Station of the Cross depicting St. Veronica wiping the face of Jesus had also been donated by our family; it even carried a plaque which stated this. We were quite taken with ourselves.

Paw-Paw had his rituals. He belonged to the parish chapter of the Holy Name Society, and one Sunday a month would sit with the other members at the front of the church during the 8:00 Mass. Afterward, he'd attend the Society's breakfast meeting. At home, he'd smoke his weekly cigar and have his Sunday highball.

Paw-Paw religiously worked the crossword puzzle and the word scramble that appeared every day in the newspaper, and that may have been how he kept his mind sharp until he died. He would sit on the living room sofa, smoking his pipe, deeply engrossed in the solutions. He never asked anyone for help. You never heard him say, "What's a five-letter word that means..." He must have rightfully assumed that if he didn't know it, neither would any of the rest of us.

When he was home for lunch, he would listen to the noontime soap operas that were broadcast over the radio, but his real interest was in the commercials. A pitchman for a liquid detergent talked about "soaking your hands in hot dish water". Paw-Paw thought that the man pronounced the word "hands" so that it sounded like the word "heads." He was right, and would point this out if anyone else was in the room. This was before the days of shooting off an irate email to the sponsor, an activity that we're certain Paw-Paw would have relished.

He answered the phone by reciting our phone number. When our telephone number was changed to one with letters in it, the new number was BR5-6029. It took awhile for Paw-Paw to quit saying "Burr 5-6029."

Every summer, Paw-Paw would spend two weeks with Uncle Jack, Aunt Cassie and their family at their home outside of Washington, D.C. He frequently had one of the Memphis grandchildren in tow. If it was your turn, you had to be prepared to spend 24 hours in a passenger car on the Tennessean, the train that ran between Memphis and Washington, because Paw-Paw thought that paying for a sleeping car was a waste of money.

The train departed Union Station in Memphis at 8:00 a.m. It made frequent stops, and arrived in Bristol, Tennessee sometime in the middle of the night to take on extra cars. The train would jounce and crash around, and anyone in the passenger cars who'd actually managed to get to sleep would be jerked rudely awake. Anyone, of course, except Paw-Paw, who routinely slept soundly through the whole jarring procedure.

The grandchild-in-tow also had to be prepared to walk all over Washington, since Paw-Paw did his sightseeing on foot and expected his companions to do the same. It didn't seem to occur to him as he loped along that our short legs had to move twice as fast to keep up with his long ones.

The year Michele went, Paw-Paw had lined up what for him was a days' worth of monuments and museums to visit. Michele, Paw-Paw and Jim Adler, the second-oldest of Uncle Jack and Aunt Cassie's kids, hit the trail. Though at ages 8 and 11 Michele and Jim were old enough to know better, they decided that it would be great fun to walk down all 898 steps of the Washington Monument. Even Paw-Paw balked at that one, and neither Jim nor Michele realized that this was because he had no intention of curtailing his planned walking tour of Washington. And he didn't, turning a deaf ear to their exhausted pleas to call it a day.

He loved Washington's art galleries, and loved pointing out the various works to us. One of his favorite pieces was a sculpture at the Corcoran Gallery of Art, called The Veiled Nun. It was a marble bust, and carved so masterfully that the veil appeared to float over the woman's face. Paw-Paw gave us our first overview of art, which was more detailed than most college art appreciation courses are.

We're not sure just when Paw-Paw began to work for the Community Chest, an organization which coordinated the charitable contributions of local businesses and which was a forerunner of the United Way in Memphis. Adrienne remembers him as being already engaged in this work when she was small. He commuted on foot, and always came home for lunch. He rarely drove a car, not because he couldn't, but because he preferred to walk.

He was forced to take a hiatus from work in the late 1940's. The family had been sitting at dinner one warm summer evening, when suddenly Daddy yelled, "Fire!" pointing toward the living room and lurching out of his chair. The ancient celluloid lampshade that crowned an old floor lamp had suddenly burst into flames. Paw-Paw, whose view of the lamp was blocked but whose chair was closer to it, didn't hesitate. He jumped up, ran in and grabbed the burning lamp, took it through the fortunately open front door and threw it over the side of the porch. There, it burned itself out harmlessly. However, Paw-Paw had second and a few third-degree burns all over both his arms.

One of his favorite activities when he retired was to take long walks around Memphis every afternoon, looking for evidence of disrepair. If he saw a pothole, a wall with new graffiti on it or a crumbling sidewalk, he'd make a mental note. On arriving home, he'd call the appropriate agency, inform them of the problem and demand that it be corrected. If the agency didn't respond quickly enough to suit him, he'd keep complaining until he received satisfaction.

He was diagnosed with laryngeal cancer in 1960. For many months, he'd been clearing his throat of what were obviously increasingly copious secretions. When he finally went to the doctor about it, the cancer was advanced. The surgery to remove the cancer left him mute and with his larynx open. It was painful to watch him.

The times were changing rapidly. Prior to his surgery, he told Nana that he was glad his days were numbered, saying that he was aghast at the upheaval he was seeing in the world.

Since Paw-Paw couldn't talk, he had been given a Magic Slate. He could write what he wanted to say, then erase it with a quick pull on the tablet. It's a credit to his genes that he maintained his sanity, never slipping into dementia. Shortly before he died, he had written on the Magic Slate, "All my love, Jim" to Nana. In his last days, he also expressed his appreciation and admiration of his daughter. "You're the best," he wrote to Aunt Dokey.

It wasn't until the week before he died that Nana snapped out of her denial to realize that the man who'd been her husband for 57 years was really going away. She was distraught, awash in a flood of memories. Sobbing, she told Michele, "The hardest thing I ever had to do was to ask him if we could bring Aunt Ding in and raise her, since we already had four children. He was fine with it, loved Ding and always thought of her as one of his own."

The sassy twenty-something who had not wanted anything to do with "skinny Jim Adler" now realized the depth of her love and appreciation for him, and that he had been the backbone of her whole life.

He always said he wouldn't leave Poplar Street except feet first. That's how he went, weighing less than 90 pounds and ravaged with cancer that couldn't be arrested with the technology available in 1963. The strong stoic soul in his Tom-Wolfe white suit with his Panama hat and his gold watch chain was gone forever. The man who said he would die when he could no longer walk had expired just a week after he was unable to get out of bed.

Technically, it was pneumonia that had killed him. The morning of Paw-Paw's death, Daddy said to Michele, "The doctors say that pneumonia is an enemy to the young..." And then, weeping, "but a friend to the old."

Someone once said that the measure of any life is what can't be taken away from it. Education and experience, of course, fall into that category, but these are the ingredients of a resume or an obituary, not a life.

Others will say that the measure of a life is what a person is willing to die for, and while that's a profound statement of courage and commitment, it's not the measure of a life.

Still others measure a life by consensus among the survivors and descendants as to what constituted that life's most important aspect. But our lives are far too complex to be left up to a vote based on one facet of our existence.

We were talking about this recently, and finally agreed that the measure of a life is the extent to which we use our gifts and fight our dragons to fulfill what-ever our purpose on earth might be, and the extent to which we grace and improve the lives of others. That's a final judgment no human can make; it can only be issued in the divine realm. Still, we think that God would forgive us for passing judgment anyway: Nana and Paw-Paw had lives that measured well.

They lived during a period of history that saw human affairs change more in 100 years than they had in the previous 1000. Through it all, Nana and Paw-Paw maintained their values, and we are all better for it. We hope they would think us worthy to be called their grandchildren.

For themselves, we suspect they would probably be content to see their legacy echoed in the utter simplicity of the Christina Rosetti poem that Paw-Paw loved.

And if thou wilt, remember.

May their souls sleep gently, safe in the knowledge that we will never forget.

MOTHER AND DADDY

Margaret Weber Adler and James Kevitt Adler

Daddy was the last of Nana and Paw-Paw's four children to marry, but our grandparents would never be empty-nesters. He brought his bride—Mother—to the house in 1940 with the idea that they would live there until they found a place of their own. After thirty-nine years and four children, they were still there, having become empty-nesters themselves.

During the 1970's, a popular television show called *The Waltons* depicted three generations of family living under the same roof. As idealized on TV, all was warm and wonderful, but in real life the situation is considerably more complicated. The negative aspects of their multigenerational dynamic presumably challenged the Waltons only during the commercials. They affected us on a daily basis as our lives played out on Poplar Street.

The Waltons lived in much slower times, when circumstances, attitudes and fundamental values didn't change dramatically from one generation to another. The Adlers dwelling at 1234 Poplar were the products of times that ranged from the days of gaslights and the horse-and-buggy to the days of manned space flight. The profound social changes that accompanied this race through time produced worldviews in the three generations that were frequently in opposition, and conflict was inevitable.

Add to this the equally inevitable conflict that ensues when a man's wife and his mother occupy the same turf, and the end result was a state of almost constant tension. Mountains were regularly constructed from molehills. Things that should have remained unsaid were shouted from the rooftops, and things that should have been said were stifled. Occasionally there would be an epic blow-up, generally during dinner and generally fueled by an extra pre-dinner cocktail or two.

We four children became accustomed to all the drama. In its absence, we felt almost dislocated. When Daddy and Mother would take us away on vacation, it didn't take us long to begin snarling at one another, which we rarely did otherwise. When Nana and Paw-Paw left for a two-week stay at Miami Beach's Fontainebleau Hotel in 1956, a 50th anniversary gift from their children, we were at each other's throats by the end of the first week. The dynamic which we'd all absorbed had imploded. Adrienne pinpointed it: "I miss Nana!" she said.

On the positive side, there was never a dull moment. We were constantly surrounded by extended family, and formed bonds of affection with our cousins and with each other that remain strong to this day. We have been privileged to enjoy one of God's loveliest gifts: that of being related to so many people whom we would have otherwise chosen for friends.

OUR PARENTS

> *"More things are wrought by prayer than this world dreams of."* – Alfred Lord Tennyson, *Morte d'Arthur*, which Mother quoted frequently.

> *"How can there be bread in the house and no whiskey?"* – Daddy, who liked Tennyson but had his priorities

All of us wonder what our parents must have been like before they had us. We gradually form images of them based upon both the remembrances that they share over the years and our own observations of them, and these images evolve throughout our lives as we grow into our own maturity.

Our mother was born Margaret Weber, and frequently reminded us that she was the second-oldest of ten children. She had seen marriage at its worst, and had no interest in getting married herself. Her brothers and sisters would laugh about the time she came home from boarding school at the Ursuline Academy and heard that another baby was on the way. "Three more years of hard work!" she exclaimed. It was said that when she came home from work to find out that the tenth child, Uncle Gene, was due, her first reaction was to break down and cry.

Having reared most of her younger siblings, she was convinced that "At age three, they're raised."

After high school, she took a position with Standard Oil in Memphis, a forerunner of Exxon. Her work had been so outstanding that she was made head of the auditing department; she'd scored higher than anyone else on a test that was given to eligible employees. In an age when women were almost never promoted to managerial positions in the workplace, she was.

Then, in the early 1930's she met Daddy.

They met at the Catholic Club in Memphis, the chief social venue of its day for the city's young Catholic men and women. Daddy was directing a play which was being produced by a group called the Young Ladies Institute, to which Mother belonged.

She soon became a part of Daddy's "crowd". In 1934, they served as the Catholic Club's Prince and Princess in the annual gala that was Cotton Carnival, now a considerably pared down and service-oriented Carnival Memphis. The original event, Memphis's answer to Mardi Gras, consisted of a week-long round of parties and parades that began at ten a.m. and frequently went on until dawn. Legend had it that if a romantic relationship survived Cotton Carnival, the couple would be together for life.

It did, and they were.

They were engaged for five years, from 1935 until their wedding in 1940. We were always told it was "the depression, and everything was bleak." As it turned out, the real reason was based upon a story that Daddy had probably concocted out of thin air and that Mother had probably pretended to believe.

After Daddy's death, Mother revealed that when she'd first met him, he'd told her that he was dying. He'd said that he had a "floating blood clot", and that the doctors had told him that it would eventually hit his heart and he'd die. It was an odd thing to tell a woman he'd just met. It was even odder that, as he claimed, his parents didn't know.

It must have been a hell of a pick-up line that had yielded prodigious results, so it's not surprising that our parents may have been reluctant to share this tidbit with their impressionable offspring.

Mother, however strong the stench of rat might or might not have been, took charge of the matter—or at least made a show of doing so. Always keenly aware of the power of prayer, she decided they would attend the Tuesday night novenas to Our Lady of Perpetual Help held at Sacred Heart Church. Remarkably, Daddy went, though it's also possible that

Mother had simply hoisted him on his own petard while continuing to pretend that they had "no future" together.

Michele doubts that Mother was capable of imagining that someone would make up such a story, and she was very somber when telling Michele about it. Adrienne thinks that she saw right through it, wanted him anyway, and was determined to play along with his act for however long it took. Which begs the question—do any two people ever see their parents the same way?

Sure enough, Daddy eventually announced that he was miraculously cured of the clot. If nothing else, the novenas had cured him of his established pattern of serial infatuations.

He gave Mother an engagement ring with a small diamond, which he later replaced with a larger one. Kevitt gave Diane Waggener the earlier stone when they became engaged, carrying on the family tradition by also replacing it later with a larger one.

Mother carried the blood clot story with her all her life, and never told any of us about it until after Daddy died. When we suggested that perhaps it was his way of stringing her along, she just smiled.

By the time they finally married on May 25, 1940, Mother and Daddy were so embarrassed about their ages that they lied on the marriage certificate—saying they were actually two years YOUNGER than they really were. In truth, she was 29. He was 31.

After thinking that he'd gotten away with the blood clot line, Daddy may have figured that it was only a small stretch to get Mother to believe they would live with Nana and Paw-Paw for a little while and then get their own place later.

So Mother and Daddy began married life at 1234 Poplar. Thirty-nine years later, they were still there. It's a tribute to them both that we can laugh about so much of it now.

MOTHER

Daddy once said that he married Mother because she was "calm and steady" and he was always "wild and woolly." In retrospect, he gave her glamour. She gave him character.

The contrast was best illustrated in a memorable story from their later years. The Poplar Street house had its share of unusual occurrences, and it was thought by some of us to be haunted. One night, Daddy and Mother woke up to distinctly hear Daddy's name being called from the first floor of the house. Always ready for a good fight, Daddy grabbed his gun and began charging downstairs to confront whatever entity was summoning him. Mother made an attempt to steer Daddy away from God-knows-what.

"Kev," she cried after him, "don't shoot it if it knows your name!"

There are a number of things that come to mind when we remember Mother. She was very shy. She was very artistic. She was very practical. She was very religious. She was very wise.

As Chris observed, Mother had three universal remedies for any crisis, and one would always work:

1) Rub it.
2) Put a Band-aid on it.
3) Say a rosary.

Saying a rosary was the weapon of choice in her arsenal, and she saw married life and raising a family as being impossible without completing at least three daily laps around the beads.

"If you say a rosary every day, you may come to the edge of the cliff, but you won't go over," she once said. And when we'd start indulging in our orgies of self-pity, she would be near at hand to bark: "Thank God for your blessings!"

Mother's devotion to Our Lady of Perpetual Help went back some years, pre-dating even the Tuesday night Floating Blood Clot Novenas.

At the height of the Depression in the 1930s, Mother was very worried that her father, Grandpa Weber, might not be able to find work. So she made

a promise to Our Lady of Perpetual Help that if he
located a job, she'd create a little shrine to her. He
did, and she kept her promise. For many years, there
was a small grotto at Immaculate Conception Church
in Memphis in which had been embedded a picture
of Our Lady of Perpetual Help. Grandpa Weber had
built the grotto using rock crystals, and later Mother
had added ceramic roses which she'd made herself. The
shrine was removed when the Church became the dioc-
esan Cathedral some years later.

Despite her strong faith, it was an ongoing struggle for Mother to accept that marriage to Daddy meant
living at 1234 Poplar for her entire married life, in a
house that wasn't hers and would never be. It meant
having responsibility for that house without having
authority over it. By the time Mother was expecting
Adrienne, it had become obvious to her that Daddy
didn't want to leave the home to which he was so
attached. In Kevitt's words, he was the father who
couldn't quit being the son. So Poplar Street became
a sticking point for our parents from the early stages
of their marriage: She wanted them to have a place of
their own, and he didn't.

In her more despairing moments, she would advise,
"Marry a rich, Catholic orphan."

However, her loyalty to Daddy was so fierce that she
developed a narrative she could live with: that his parents
were somehow forcing him to stay there. It was only in
her twilight years that she came to realize that this was
not the case. "They were good people," she told Michele.

In hindsight, we think that Nana and Paw-Paw would have been relieved to see Daddy and his sourpuss collection of human baggage move out. There's no way they could have welcomed the treatment that they too often received from us children as a result of Mother's inability to keep her theories to herself. Nana once told us, "Someday, you'll be sorry." She was so right. It's someday now, and we are. We're also grateful that we were able to enjoy and appreciate our grandparents as much as we did under the circumstances.

Mother was steadfast in her adherence to the idea that the more education you had, the better off you would be. She had a horror that her daughters would one day have to support themselves, and her ace-in-the-hole was to get them well-schooled enough to permit this. Still, she wanted to allow for all contingencies, so she embraced the Southern tradition of beginning immediate preparations for a newborn girl's future marriage by starting the infant a silver pattern.

When we were babies—BABIES, for God's sake— the word subtly went out to anyone who might be disposed to give us a present that our silver pattern was Wallace's *Rose Point*. The utensils were engraved on the back with our initials, but a space was left "for the initial of the man you marry." Naturally, we were frequently disappointed when it was time to open gifts. What kid wants to get a spoon for a present? Adrienne finally appreciated the value of this tradition when she married on three days' notice. She would have to get her own china and crystal later, but she had a full silver service for eight already on hand.

Mother was determined that our dormant talents be ferreted out and nurtured. She saw that both of us studied music, and presented seven-year old Michele with the old manual typewriter on which Michele first began developing a writing ability that served her well in her later career.

One summer, Mother enrolled Michele in a typing and shorthand course at Miller-Hawkins, an institution down the street run by two elderly ladies. Michele's ability to type 90 words per minute using the hunt-and-peck system didn't impress anyone, but by the time she left, she could do 125 wpm while using the correct typing techniques. She was considered a prodigy, if there can be such a thing in a typing class, and Mother knew peace at last: Michele had at least one skill that could be useful if she needed to support herself.

Mother was a gifted artist. When she was in her seventies, one of her paintings took a first-place award at the Tennessee State Fair, even though it wasn't until later in life that she'd taken up acrylics. She especially loved ceramics, and many of her works grace the homes of family members throughout the country. Each Christmas, Adrienne and Kevitt display the ceramic Nativity sets that Mother created for them all those years ago. There is a statue in front of Immaculate Conception Cathedral in Memphis with a circle on the ground below it that contains ceramic tiles that she made.

Her daughters did not inherit this particular strand of DNA. Mother enrolled both of us in classes at the

Memphis Academy of Arts, but Michele was lacking in artistic talent and Adrienne was bored with having to draw still life arrangements WITHOUT the worm coming out of the apple. We were dropouts after two weeks. The arts caper brought about one of Daddy's few dictums. "I don't want to hear anything more about art lessons," he averred.

Mother always encouraged us to achieve. Her favorite admonition was, "You haven't BEGUN to scratch your potential!"

Chris, who mightily resisted any push he didn't specifically request, would respond, "I'm supposed to scratch my potential in public?"

Sometimes it got embarrassing for Mother. She had signed both of us up for dancing lessons, another non-starter, when we were quite young. During Adrienne's classes, Mother and Michele would watch from the sidelines. One day, Adrienne's teacher addressed the group, saying that she felt very tired, and hoped they would all behave because she was having a very bad day.

Michele decided the woman would appreciate feed-back. "What you need," she proclaimed at the top of her four-year-old voice, "is a slug of whiskey!"

All the other mothers turned and stared aghast at Mother, who was mortified. This was in Memphis, the heart of the Bible belt, in the late 1940's, where no one drank or dared to admit it if they did.

Mother went home and wailed to Daddy about this awful thing Michele had said. Daddy, on the other hand, thought Michele's advice was on target. "Sounds like a slug of whiskey was just what the woman needed!" he opined.

That was one of the things Mother liked about Daddy. He would turn everything into a joke, at which point she could stop stewing and fretting about whatever it was and start laughing instead.

She loved short-cuts. Her goal was always to achieve as much as possible while doing as little as possible. She also displayed an economy of physical movement, evidenced strikingly in her tennis serve. Mother successfully competed in local tournaments, not because of her strength or her swiftness of foot, but because no opponent could return that serve.

The only time we ever saw it was when she joined us for the occasional badminton game. The shuttlecock always looked as though it would fall before clearing the net, but it didn't. Instead, it would make a little vertical hairpin-like move that would just barely propel it over, leaving her opponent startled. The key was that the opponent always thought it was a fluke, and then she duplicated the strange serve, again and again.

She took the same minimalist approach to infant care. The family crib was a death trap that for some unfathomable reason had been designed with a bowed head and foot. Since the mattress was rectangular, this left a crescent-shaped gap at either end of the crib, through which all of us, as babies, fell at least once. Nowadays, the crib would have been put on the recall list and never sold anywhere again, with its manufacturer charged with attempted infanticide and forced out of business. But this was the late 1940's.

At feeding time, the infant would be laid in the crib, its bottle propped up on a stack of diapers and its head turned in the general direction of this edifice. In the process of squirming and rooting toward sustenance, the baby would occasionally take a wrong turn and wind up as a human sacrifice to the gap.

After Chris was born, Mother got the idea of stuffing the gaps with pillows, but for the rest of us it had given a whole new meaning to things falling through the cracks.

Mother found new ways of implementing her low-effort-high-efficiency approach even when we were adults. In the 1970s, Michele would write long, typed letters home during her stints in various cities where she worked. Mother obviously didn't want to write long letters back. To lessen her guilt, she bought note cards instead of letter-size stationery, then filled them with out-sized script. It was a Vintage Mother solution.

Adrienne disagrees with Michele's observation that Mother hated to cook. Adrienne thinks she just lost all interest because of having to cook the same old things over and over lest somebody set up a howl. Still, it was a good thing that she only had to perform on Thursdays, when the maid was off. She would use every pot in the kitchen with total abandon, since cleaning up the mess was our job, not hers.

One night, Chris observed that he finally understood Mother's system: Keep the rice moving at all costs. He pointed out that there were three pots that had rice in them, possibly a result of Mother's irritation at having to use more than one cooking temperature.

Thursday nights in the kitchen became a ritual of sorts. Daddy would sit and watch Mother cook. We children would just gather around and babble. One evening, Kevitt posed a riddle: "A man is lying in the field with a pack on his back, and he's dead. How did he die?" We ventured guesses, all of them wrong. Mother was stirring something on the stove. She said, "His parachute didn't open." We were all agog that Mother, neither a reader nor academically oriented, would be the one to guess correctly. Kevitt was sitting on the edge of the old farm-type sink that we had in the kitchen, and was so astonished that he fell into it.

Mother would short-cut and alter recipes to the point where the dish was unrecognizable. She'd leave out ingredients that she thought were too expensive, too hard to find or too uninspiring, and substitute ones that were more to her liking. As adults, we developed an interest in cooking, and would occasionally send Mother recipes for concoctions that had gone over well when we served them to friends.

We needn't have bothered. Her version of Michele's storied sautéed mushrooms prompted Daddy to comment, "Is this what all the fuss was about?" Adrienne's peanut soup also bombed. When Mother told a disgruntled Daddy that "Adrienne said her guests asked for more of this soup instead of dessert," Daddy retorted that the guests must have been out-of-their-minds drunk.

One Sunday evening, Chris made a terse observation: "Mom can't cook." He was staring at a hamburger she'd fixed for him, which bore a striking resemblance to a desiccated cow pie.

Housework held no charms for Mother either; blessed with a succession of maids at Poplar Street, she rarely had to do much of it besides our laundry. Even that was occasionally problematic, as exemplified by the time that she apparently failed to notice that she'd thrown a red shirt into the washing machine along with her husband's and sons' underwear. They did not take kindly to their new pink lingerie.

On the other hand, she loved to sew and was an accomplished seamstress. When she was pregnant with Kevitt, she spent much of her time sewing a christening gown, which was exquisite, and worn by all of her grandchildren at their christenings. Made of fine cotton batiste, it featured multiple rows of lace and ribbon beading that she'd sewn by hand. Mother later attributed Kevitt's intense attention to detail to her own obsession with the christening dress during his gestation.

Executing Adrienne's designs always brought out the best of her creative talents. One Halloween, Adrienne had been invited to a costume party and decided that she and her date were going as "space cadets". Mother had saved her own Cotton Carnival costume, which featured an Egyptian motif and fairly dripped gold trim. Mother scavenged the gold and recycled it into appropriately other-worldly costumes, for which Adrienne and her date won first prize.

Adrienne's Fashion Muse was frequently activated on the spur of the moment. Instead of telling Adrienne and her Muse where they could go and how fast they could do it, Mother hustled to oblige them. This generally meant a fair amount of last-minute work on her part.

So one day, the sewing machine was moved from its customary place in Mother's and Daddy's bedroom into Poplar Street's second floor bathroom. That way, Mother could work far into the night without disturbing Daddy's sleep. The sight of the machine and the yards of fabric draped over the bathtub elicited some frankly curious stares from the various tradesmen who came upon it. To Mother's credit and Adrienne's dismay, Mother finally grew a spine and drew a line at making a wedding dress for her daughter two days before the ceremony.

We were fortunate that Mother's talents included taking apart clothes that we loved but which were no longer fit to wear and then making patterns from the pieces. Given our champagne tastes on beer budgets, having a collection of skirts and slacks that fit perfectly was a windfall.

Mother tried to keep her presence muted if she thought we were studying, lest she intrude upon what passed for our mental concentration. Unfortunately, her self-effacing tippy-toeing around was highly distracting. One night, Adrienne was cramming for a medical school exam. Mother was gathering up laundry, skulking about and trying hard not to disturb her. Finally, in exasperation, Adrienne snapped, "Mother, would you PLEASE quit sluefooting around?" The name quickly took hold. From then on, we called her Sluefoot. One day, she dropped Chris off at school. He was about 10 feet out when he remembered that he'd left something in the car. So at the top of his voice, he yelled "Sluefoot! Wait!" Though she'd grown fond of her new nickname, it wasn't something she wanted the world to know.

Her common sense was unrivaled when it wasn't clouded with worry or paranoia, or overwhelmed by the incomprehensible—as it was on the morning of April 29, 1944. On that beautiful spring day, Mother was making the beds in the upstairs back bedroom with Adrienne ostensibly helping. Suddenly, they heard the very loud and very close roar of an airplane. Mother cried, "Get under the bed!", theorizing that if the plane hit the house, the ceiling would cave in on the mattress and bounce off.

She might as well have saved her breath. Adrienne was frozen with fear; to this day, she vividly recalls the open doors leading to the balcony, framing the image of a plane with an engine on fire hurtling downward not far above the roof of the garage. It cleared the trees and disappeared from view, and then there was a deafening crash. Adrienne, Mother and Nana ran outside to see a huge plume of smoke and fire rising from the neighborhood on the other side of Tech High. Adrienne was later told that everyone in the plane and in the house into which it crashed had been killed. Even at the age of not-quite-three, she'd already figured out that getting under the bed wouldn't have helped.

But Mother had elevated worrying to an art form. When she married, her sister, Aunt Mary Frances, sent her a worry bird as a gift. However, when WE worried, she would say, "Half the things you worry about never happen."

We inferred from this that the more you worried about something, the less likely it was to happen. We developed a protocol:

Step 1: Decide what all could go wrong in a given circumstance. Be creative.

Step 2: Taking each possible scenario, mentally leap smack into the middle of it, and envision all the gruesomeness.

Step 3: Wallow in the wreckage! Feel the pain!

Step 4: At the point of utter hopelessness, relax, safe in the assurance that surely God wouldn't punish you with the real thing after all that suffering.

Even in her 80's, Mother would occasionally ask strangers, "If you tell a child that half the things they worry about will never happen, would you think that would make them worry even harder?" This always mystified her. To us it made perfect sense.

Mother was unable to sleep when Adrienne was out on a date. She'd lie awake, making her way around her rosary, until the slam of the front door announced that the prodigal daughter had returned. If Adrienne was late, Mother would first wake Michele, whose duty it was to commiserate and to share the worry load. Michele could never get properly attuned to Mother's panic, knowing full well that Adrienne, like Lassie, always came home eventually.

The years of worry had to have taken their toll. Michele once asked Mother when in her life she had been happiest. Her answer was immediate: *"When I was on my own, single, earning my own money."* Then, suddenly realizing that she was talking to her daughter, she attempted an about-face. "Oh, when you children came along. That's when I was happiest!" Mother was not very good at un-ringing a bell.

Yet her legacy went far deeper than worrying and making us clothes. In retrospect, she showed us that even the most loving commitment is not without its price. She would always say that there "was no such thing as a perfect situation." But we sensed, Poplar Street notwithstanding, that she had come close. At the end of her life, Mother had only one thought. "I just want to be with Kev," she said.

DADDY

> *"The boast of heraldry, the pomp of power,*
> *And all that beauty, all that wealth e'er gave;*
> *Await alike the inevitable hour,*
> *The paths of glory lead but to the grave."*

> - Thomas Gray, *Elegy Written in a Country Churchyard,* Daddy's favorite stanza from his favorite poem

One muggy June day in Memphis in 2003, our nephew Kev gave the valedictory address at White Station High School in Memphis. Kev is Kevitt and Diane Adler's extraordinary son, the second person to carry Daddy's name, and it was a snapshot moment. Michele thought during the address how happy his grandparents would have been to see and hear Kev on his graduation day. At the moment of her thought, Kev happened to recite the last line of the stanza of a poem that he didn't know was a favorite of his grandfather: *"The paths of glory lead but to the grave."*

Daddy would quote it on occasion, and then tell us about General James Wolfe. Wolfe had recited the entire poem for his troops the night before he died leading the victorious British assault against the French in Quebec City in 1759. Wolfe, Daddy said, told his

troops he'd rather have written those lines than taken
Quebec. We got the impression that Daddy felt a kin-
ship with James Wolfe, a warrior who shared his taste
in poetry.

Daddy would frequently use great literature to
assuage some childhood trauma. If we were unusually
afraid of something, he would say, "The coward dies
many times before his death. The valiant taste of it
but once." It was a line from Act ll of Shakespeare's
Julius Caesar, and if nothing else it did help to blunt
the inadvertent message we got from Mother to worry
everything down to its molecular level.

Daddy was just as comfortable quoting literature
as he was trading stories with the denizens of the South
Memphis Stock Yards. This was where he spent much of
his time as a cattle buyer for Engelberg Packing Company, which aged, cut, trimmed and packaged beef for
wholesale. Daddy was devoted to "Pop" Engelberg, the
founder of the company. He worked with Pop's sons:
Jake, Harry, Izzy, and Reuben. When Pop Engelberg
had leukemia, Daddy accompanied him to Rochester,
Minnesota for his treatments at the Mayo Clinic. Pop
Engelberg died in the early 1950s, and for Daddy it
was like losing a second father.

Aunt Dokey said that Daddy was "always Nana's
favorite." In truth, he was just like Nana's father,
Michael Reedy, whom Nana idolized. In Daddy's later
years, Uncle Dut said of him: "He not only looks like
Grandpa Reedy, he acts like him." Mother recalled
Nana once saying that Daddy was just like her. "I

didn't see it then, but I do now," Mother said shortly before Daddy died.

Daddy went to Sacred Heart grammar school, as did all of us up until Adrienne's high school graduation, and his reputation for being "wild and woolly" was cemented at a relatively early age. He remembered that one of his first fights had been at Sacred Heart when some bully tried to rough up Uncle Dut, who was two years younger than he was. Daddy said he only remembered going into a rage and attacking the kid, and vaguely recalled the nuns hitting him with their umbrellas to prevent Daddy from killing him.

He was always a scrapper who was fond of declaring, "The meek shall inherit the earth...six feet of it." It was evident that he'd given serious thought to some other Biblical quotations that were relevant to his fighting spirit. "The Lord says if someone hits you to turn the other cheek," Daddy once observed. Then, smiling triumphantly, he would add: "But the Lord never said what to do if they hit that one!"

When Adrienne was small, she recalls standing in the front seat of Daddy's car one frigid New Year's morning while Daddy drove around downtown Memphis in search of the guy who'd bested him in a fistfight the night before. She was glad that they didn't find the Bad Man.

Even in his late sixties, with the Poplar Street neighborhood becoming unsafe and the elderly being easy prey, Daddy stayed true to his nature. There was a miscalculation or two on the part of some local thugs, who were forced to flee when Daddy came at them with the tire iron he'd resorted to carrying.

At the age of ten, Daddy was unceremoniously shipped off to join Uncle Jack at St. Mary's, a Jesuit boarding school near Topeka, Kansas, which has long since closed its doors. By this time, Nana was intent upon pursuing a possible career as an opera singer, and did not welcome the distraction of her obstreperous sons.

At St. Mary's, Daddy found himself the smallest boy in the school. Consequently, there were attempts by some of the older and bigger boys to surreptitiously bully him.

These attempts were sadly misguided.

The priests at St. Mary's had a rule that any of the boys caught fighting would participate that evening in the nightly boxing matches, which represented the school's version of anger management. When lining up for morning Mass, Daddy would pick out one of the bullies, go up to the boy, and slug him in full view of the Jesuit proctor. The two boys would then be ordered to box that night, and Daddy invariably won. He may have been small, but he was quick, he was strong, he was coordinated, and he was very, very determined.

Daddy boxed every night for a month. After that, nobody messed with him.

His St. Mary's years provided him with stories for the rest of his life. He was a talented athlete, playing all sports, but he particularly liked football. In his senior year of high school he and several of his teammates were recruited by the legendary coach Knute Rockne to play football at Notre Dame.

They decided instead to stay and play for St. Mary's college, thinking somewhat grandiosely that if they were good enough for Notre Dame, they could put St. Mary's on the football map. But when Paw-Paw was facing bankruptcy during the Great Depression, Daddy had to come home after only two years of college. That was the end of his formal education.

Even so, it was quite an impressive education, of the sort no longer found in America's secondary schools. What was taught Daddy in high school was the equivalent of at least a full college education today, with four years of both Latin and Greek having been required of all students. Daddy once mentioned to Kevitt about having taken some courses at the University of Memphis, then known as State Teachers College, and reflected on how easy it had been compared to St. Mary's.

As a young man, Daddy was in the center of an active social set that reflected the energy of the times. He was strikingly handsome, and projected an aura of glamour. Even after he and Mother married, they would go out for the evening every Thursday on what would now be called "date night". Though these evenings out became sporadic after their children were born, we recall their occasional attendance at formal events. When Daddy would come down Poplar Street's main staircase and we'd tell him what a good-looking tuxedo he was wearing, he'd correct us: "It's a good-looking man *wearing* it!"

He also had some acting ability, and performed in several productions at Memphis' Little Theatre. One was a production of *Hell Bent for Heaven* which featured a scene where he was supposed to come on stage after swimming, clad in a bathing suit. Every night, someone would pour water on him so that he could make his entrance appropriately drenched. This was Memphis, in February, and he came down with pleurisy.

It was said that he'd been approached about going to Hollywood. But considering the family flair for hyperbole, it's unclear whether this would have meant being in a movie or pumping gas.

It was easy to picture him in formal dress, whirling around the dance floors of the Peabody, the Claridge, the Chisca and the King Cotton hotels. Sometimes, these gala evenings of his youth would degenerate into brawls, which he and one of his compatriots would start just for the fun of it. Needless to say, he developed a reputation for being a troublemaker, which did not have a salubrious effect on his social standing.

The Commercial Appeal once regularly ran a "Days Gone By" column, containing snippets of local news from 25, 50 and 75 years earlier. When we were teenagers, there was a "25 years ago" entry that referred to some social event attended by "the three Adler brothers." Their legend was such that there was no other identification given, or presumably needed.

While the "Days Gone By" snippet didn't mention it, Aunt Dokey was also part of the scene. She and Uncle Dut were turning into Memphis's answer to Fred Astaire and Ginger Rogers, practicing their dance steps at Poplar Street and then heading out on the town to show them off. En route to a party one evening, Aunt Dokey and Daddy had just boarded a hotel elevator when it crashed from the lobby into the basement. Daddy was unhurt, but the resulting injury to Aunt Dokey's knee both put an end to her dancing and afflicted her for the rest of her life.

In Daddy's early twenties, he suffered a ruptured appendix, and required an emergency appendectomy. He spent ten days in the hospital, during which time he made a number of friends among the nursing staff. While he was at home recovering, Nana and Paw-Paw were called out of town. Daddy and Uncle Dut decided to take this golden opportunity to host a week-long house party, to which they invited all of Daddy's new friends—ostensibly to help Daddy recuperate. Uncle Dut regaled us with the details of the party only after his wife Aunt Leeze, who'd exerted a muzzling influence on his more colorful stories, had passed away. It was apparently a gathering that Hugh Hefner would have envied.

Occasionally, one of our childhood playmates would volunteer the information that her Mom or her

Dad knew Daddy. When we conveyed this to Daddy, he'd frequently have no memory of that person.

"But they said they knew *you*," we would say.

To which he would loftily retort, "Well, not to have known *Caesar*…"

Daddy was an avid football fan, and fairly worshiped the Fighting Irish of Notre Dame. Hearing their fight song could move him to tears. At the beginning of football season each fall, he would have the same dream: that he was young again and playing football for Knute Rockne. The Saturday afternoons of autumn found him glued to the radio and the television, listening intently for the scores and calling his bookie periodically. He claimed that Notre Dame's football victories put Adrienne through medical school, a fact of which he was quite proud.

Daddy had a long series of girl friends, and there's no doubt a story to go with many of them. But he fell seriously in love with only one of them, and that was Mother.

One of Daddy's courting habits was to go to the lobby of the Peabody Hotel and write love letters to Mother. Mother kept those letters for over sixty years. She finally destroyed them a few years before she died, only because she considered the letters deeply private and was repelled by the thought that anyone else would read them. However, she retained one, and gave it and two letters he wrote her from Rochester in 1948 to Michele.

Daddy's hot-headedness must have been problematic for Mother during their courtship. In the only surviving Peabody letter dated April, 1934, he apologized to her for an outburst the previous evening. He acknowledged his temper, but also that he loved her and was going to marry her. Until "that happy day," he wrote, "be generous and forgiving to your Mr. Cabbage, who needs your love more than you'll ever know." The "Mr. Cabbage" signature referred to a name one of the Peabody bell men had given him, since everyone outside the family struggled to remember "Kevitt."

The letters were an interesting trip back in time, but Michele didn't understand why Daddy was writing them at the Peabody. "All the young men did that," Mother said. "They'd go to the Peabody lobby and write love letters on Peabody stationery."

All the fine young men.

Daddy loved his bourbon. Along with everybody else who knew him, Mother's parents were aware of this and were apprehensive that she might be marrying an alcoholic. Daddy's response to their concerns was to give up booze for Lent and not even allow himself a dispensation on St. Patrick's Day or Sundays, when it was acceptable to fudge on your Lenten penance. It was Aunt Mary Frances who commented: "We figured if he didn't drink during Lent, he wasn't a real alcoholic!" Daddy, in the interests of preserving this illusion, observed the Lenten abstinence ritual every year thereafter.

He loved kids, loved surrounding himself with them, and felt most at home among them—probably because he was, at heart, a kid himself. He said once that he even wanted to adopt some, but Mother wasn't game for that, so it didn't happen. Daddy doted on his nieces and nephews, to whom we were close. Even today, our cousins recall him hauling all of us to ice skating shows and circuses. Bill Rowe remembers the spotlight on Daddy's old Dodge, and how he'd shine it on the doors of the kids' homes when he dropped them off after these events to make sure they could see to get inside.

Carol Rowe attributes her status as the fourth grade's top seller of Girl Scout Cookies to Daddy, who'd take cases of them to the stock yards and hawk them. The scout leader would struggle to keep him supplied.

Daddy's co-workers must have wearily accepted their roles as targets for the fund-raising efforts of the schools and organizations to which his children, nieces and nephews belonged. They got a break when we sold World's Finest Chocolate, the bait of choice used by Sacred Heart in its annual fund drive. We usually ate our allotted supply before Daddy could peddle it.

Thanks to his stock yard connections, Daddy was the go-to guy when Science Fair projects came due. One of Carol's entries, *The Eye as a Camera,* featured cow eyeballs he'd procured.

One Christmas, Carol's teacher had the class memorize Luke 2:1-10, the gospel telling of the birth of Christ. The children were to recite it to their parents as a special Christmas gift. Her father, our Uncle Marine, was so impressed that he insisted she also recite it for Daddy, who rewarded her with a hug and a five-dollar bill. This represented a small fortune to Carol.

As a toddler, Mimi Rowe Besterczei lived at 1234 Poplar for a time while Aunt Dokey and Uncle Marine were in Baltimore. She came to call Daddy "Papa Kev," and the name stuck with the cousins. Daddy, who wanted to make sure that Mimi didn't miss out on anything at school, once gave her the money for a class trip to Shiloh and Pickwick Dam when her own father decided the family couldn't afford the fee.

As he grew older, Daddy referred to himself as "the Old Goat," in the third person. One fine spring day, he happened to see some teenagers on Montgomery Street who were blocking our driveway with their car. He admonished them for it, but as he turned away he heard one of them saying, "OK, Pops." That he would be mistaken for a "Pops" clearly marked a rite of passage for Daddy. Telling us the story, he said, "Well, the Old Goat turned around and gave them a piece of his mind!"

For one of his birthdays around that time, we bought him a sterling silver ID bracelet on which we planned to inscribe the word, "Goat". Upon further consideration, we decided that this lacked dignity and replaced it with "The Goat." In time, we would bury him with it.

Daddy and Mother gradually became empty-nesters. Adrienne had moved to Washington, D.C. in December, 1965, and was to remain there permanently following her marriage to Jim Downs a year later. Over Thanksgiving weekend of 1969 our parents saw two more of their children depart for good: Kevitt left Poplar Street to marry Diane Waggener, and Michele moved to Boston, the first in a series of her relocations. Adrienne and Jim had flown down for Kevitt's and Diane's wedding, and were driving back with Michele, who was to drop them off in Washington on her way north. We didn't realize how deeply Daddy felt about it until the three of us were ready to leave. As we began saying our goodbyes, Michele started to cry, and then *he* started to cry.

Chris was the last of us to go, in the early 1970s. After he married Susan Morris in 1978, they lived in Memphis for several years, during which time Susan worked as a news anchor and a reporter for the local Channel 13. Ironically, when 1234 Poplar was sold to Memphis House, it was Susan who covered the story from its front porch.

Over the years, Daddy had developed a facility for sidestepping emotionally fraught issues that he preferred not to confront, and focusing instead on ways to extricate himself from them. He had become quite taken with a story he'd heard about a man who was fed up with the constant aggravation of his wife and family. The man announced that he was going out for a pack of cigarettes, went out the door, and never came back. Though the story was probably an urban legend, Daddy related to it so well that whenever tensions ran high on Poplar Street, he'd say "I'm going out for cigarettes." This was code for his earnest desire to put as much distance as possible between himself and any more family drama.

He would also circle around painful subjects. A year before he died, Daddy casually told Michele that he'd just renewed his Time magazine subscription for the next five years. Michele nodded, but he pressed on, since he knew she hadn't guessed at what he was really conveying.

"I guess it's optimistic of me to be thinking I'll still be here five years from now." He paused, and then said, "I'm slowing down." It was a stark admission, unlike him.

Michele, well-schooled in joking about the inevitable, asked, "And how many race hurdles were you planning on jumping in the next five years?"

"None!" he said immediately, with all the brightness he could muster.

"Well all right then," said Michele.

When Michele told Chris the story, Chris observed that most monumental matters in this family were always closed with someone saying, "Well, all right then."

Daddy's health was an ongoing source of concern to everybody. Nana worried incessantly about him, as did

Mother. He had intractable high blood pressure, which first came to light when he had a stroke in 1964. He'd been lucky in that its only residual effects seemed to have been a mild inability to judge distances, which made riding in the passenger seat of his car a singularly hair-raising experience but was otherwise unnoticeable.

Following this episode, he very grudgingly quit smoking his three packs a day of unfiltered Camels. The cigarettes notwithstanding, he continued to keep the producers of rotgut bourbon in business until a painful attack of pancreatitis five years before his death finally put the kibosh on that practice.

These lifestyle changes weren't enough to keep his blood pressure at a safe level. He disliked the side effects of the increasingly powerful drugs required to control it almost as much as he disliked the cardiologist, whose reserved and precise demeanor stood in sharp contrast to Daddy's earthy gregariousness.

On a sweltering June day a few weeks before he died, Daddy decided to clean out the back porch closet. This closet was an airless space that became an oven in the heat of summer, and Daddy's blood pressure, already dangerously elevated, undoubtedly rose even higher as a result of the effort he expended.

Two weeks later, he had the stroke that killed him. Mother heard him call to her, and went to find him sitting on the back stairs, with Ming Toy, his Pekingnese, beside him. She telephoned Chris, who came over immediately and called the ambulance that took him away. It would be the last time he would see Poplar Street.

Following the acute onset of his symptoms, he seemed to settle down. Fully cognizant in the hospital, he reminded Mother that she was due for her hair appointment. On June 27, he mentioned to her that it was Adrienne's birthday. Then he slowly slipped into a coma.

Adrienne recalls that when Daddy was first hospitalized, she'd offered to come immediately but was told that it wasn't necessary, that he was stable—even getting better. Two days later, a distraught Mother was asking Adrienne whether to give permission for the surgery that the doctors told her was the only way to save him. She put the neurosurgeon on the phone; he informed Adrienne that Daddy had bled deep inside his brain, and that without the surgery he'd either die or remain in a permanent vegetative state.

Adrienne and Michele flew in from their respective homes in Virginia and Florida, arriving when Daddy was in surgery. Though it initially appeared that the operation had been successful, he hemorrhaged again in the recovery room, requiring a second operation. We stayed with Mother through a nightmarish evening during which we saw her dissolve. All of the fear, the frustration, and the undying love she'd always have for him came out in an explosion of grief.

Daddy never regained consciousness, and died on July 6, 1979. It may have been one of the few times that nurses in an intensive care unit could be seen crying. He'd only been there two weeks, but even a stroke couldn't dim his charm. Daddy always said that when the time came for him to leave this world, he would turn his face to the wall, and say, *"Die, you s.o.b., die!"* We like to think that even in a coma, with bandaged head and multiple tubes in place, that's what he did.

The morning after his death, we put together his burial clothes, which we assumed Mother would want to take to the funeral home. When we found her, sobbing in the living room at Poplar Street, all she said was, "I can't. I just can't." We told her we'd take care of it, and quickly handed her Adrienne's five-month-old Brian, who, even at that age, knew that his job was to cheer her up. He succeeded admirably.

At Daddy's funeral Mass, we sat through a eulogy by a priest who kept referring to him as "Mr. Adler." Everything seemed so perfunctory. It took Father Jim Harrington, a family friend who was concelebrating, to make it personal. In one of the Mass's ritual prayers, he entrusted Daddy to God with the simple words, *"Remember Kev."* Not that anyone wouldn't. Though our lives were marked forever by the fact that he refused to leave Poplar Street, we remember him with love and amusement.

Mother died 18 years later to the day, on July 6, 1997. She had colon cancer which had metastasized widely. She'd wanted to die, so much so that she'd withheld information about the extent of her disease rather than risk being subjected to chemotherapy.

"I have no idea," she told Michele, "why I am still on this earth."

Family history often seems to be a jumble of anecdotes and observations, floating in and out of context. In truth, blood really is thicker than water, but such density hampers clarity. So it is little wonder that none of us really knows our parents. We don't understand the extent to which the flotsam and jetsam of preceding generations shaped their lives. What we think we know is based on our perceptions of their words and deeds in relation to ourselves, and filtered through the prism of our own wants, needs and fears. Our images of them can get distorted as we judge how well or poorly those wants were satisfied, those needs were met, and those fears allayed.

What we actually know is that they gave us life, and that they tried to deal with who we were and their expectations of us as well as they could, given their own limitations.

Daddy taught us how to laugh. He had a strong streak of cringe-worthy foolhardiness, but we always knew he was on our side.

Mother taught us to pray, and how to endure. We've discovered that the two are closely related, which Mother knew all along. She also taught us to find peace in the Divine spark that manifests itself in the positive use of our talents and our creativity.

She said that no prayer ever goes to waste. It would take our own maturity to realize that when a prayer goes seemingly unanswered, it's because what we want is not necessarily what we need. At times, God may be sparing us the unanticipated and unintended consequences of our ill-considered requests. Or, He may be saying, "I will use the energy of these prayers you think I'm not answering, and bless you in ways you cannot possibly imagine."

And so He did.

The mystics say that the soul chooses its parents, the human beings who will enable it to fulfill its purpose. What if we had chosen others? What if we had never known Mother and Daddy? The spirit buckles at the thought of what we would have missed.

They wouldn't have missed it either: And we sense that on some alternate dawn in eternity, they both know that the paths of glory lead well beyond the grave.

PART TWO

POPLAR STREET'S ORBIT

The Shoestring Tour

Upstairs, downstairs at Poplar Street

Pets

Dogs, feral cats, birds

and a plethora of pigeons

Visitors

Fantastic cousins, psychiatric escapees

and unseen entities

A SHOESTRING TOUR OF
POPLAR STREET

The house was born in 1900, built of red brick and boasting a terra cotta tile roof. Its interior style reflected the era's embrace of the Arts and Crafts movement, with the rectilinear pattern of Mission Oak beams traversing the twelve-foot ceilings of the reception areas, the towering pocket doors that separated the living and dining rooms, the stained glass used in some of the windows, and the abundance of simply designed but flawlessly executed millwork.

It was sited at the corner of Poplar Avenue and Montgomery Street, on what had once been the Montgomery estate. We had heard that there had formerly been a swimming pool in the large lot behind the garage, but that it had been covered over and abandoned to the weeds after a child had drowned in it.

There were four fireplaces, the largest of which was in the living room. It featured a brick surround and a massive oak mantel cut from a single log, from which our Christmas stockings hung every year. When Adrienne was seven, Daddy introduced our first television set, whose minute seven-inch screen winked from a large cabinet which also accommodated a turntable and a radio. For God knows what reason, it was placed directly in front of the fireplace, shielding it from view. As our TV screens got bigger, their cabinetry got smaller, and the original console spent the rest of its life functioning as a radio or a phonograph stationed in the rear of the foyer below the open staircase landing. Its successor TV sets were much more compact, permitting them to be easily moved aside should someone get the urge to build a fire.

Above the mantel was an enormous mirror. It was positioned on a slight angle to reflect the living room and the foyer behind it, so that it wasn't necessary to turn away from the TV set to see who was coming in the front door. Or, for that matter, to see who might be breaking in the front door. Poplar Street may have been ahead of its time, unwittingly pioneering the video security systems in use today.

A second fireplace graced the dining room. It was smaller, in keeping with the scale of the room, and never used. The third one was in Nana's and Paw-Paw's bedroom; it, too, was never used except by the random pigeon that had lost its bearings. The poor creature would zoom around the house, its bowels loose with terror, until it was finally shooed out the front door.

No one could remember when the smallest fireplace had been closed off and boarded up. It was in the one room that needed it the most, the back bedroom that became Mother's and Daddy's room after their marriage. The room was surrounded on three sides by exterior walls and faced north, and during the winter was always ten degrees colder than the rest of the house. Mother developed an obsession with not being warm enough, and as she grew older would don all manner of bizarre but functional clothing and headgear in which she would face the great indoors.

The house's walls and ceilings were of plaster, which required periodic maintenance. The walls received it when their canvas coverings were repainted but the ceilings didn't, since none of us was inclined to look up and check for cracks. This oversight resulted in part of the dining room ceiling collapsing after dinner one evening, onto the chair that Daddy had just vacated. In some circles, that might be considered an omen. But on Poplar Street, it only merited curious shrugs.

Today's homebuyer would have been perplexed by the layout of the house, not realizing that it had been designed to accommodate live-in servants whose presence was to be unobtrusive.

This accounted for the seemingly wasted space consumed by the hallways, the grand front staircase separated by a wall from a second, utilitarian back one, and a wide second-floor area with cabinets and closets opening off of it.

It explained the bell box, each bell labeled with the room from which it was being rung. Though disconnected shortly after the Adlers purchased the house, it still hung on one wall of the huge, unwieldy kitchen sequestered at the back of the house, and it remained there until Poplar Street was finally sold.

The kitchen was big enough to house two refrigerators and a table which, when pulled out from its customary position against the wall, easily seated six. A butler's pantry separated the kitchen from the dining room, which was entered through a swinging door. With its marble serving counter and glass-paned cabinetry, the butler's pantry was undoubtedly an attractive space at one time. However, Daddy's additions of a deep freezer and an ungainly stand-alone bar where he held court during parties effectively masked any charm it possessed.

The kitchen sported a blue and white mosaic tile floor, which received most of the foot traffic entering and leaving the house. The extensive grouting had blackened over the years, giving the floor a decidedly unhygienic appearance which daily mopping did little to improve.

The whole area would have been a prime candidate for a design show makeover had such shows existed then. Because the space was so broken up by four doors and two large windows, there was a sparsity of cabinets in the kitchen proper.

Cooking and baking equipment was scattered haphazardly among the base cabinets, and food staples could be found either in one of the two upper cabinets or in an unheated pantry that opened off the far side of the kitchen. Dishes, glasses and flatware were housed in the butler's pantry cabinets, about fifteen feet away from the sink. When Adrienne broke down and taught herself to cook following her marriage, she was flabbergasted to discover how much an organized kitchen could simplify things.

The Havilland china, the crystal and the various antique serving pieces were kept on display in the dining room in two glass-fronted china "presses", which jingled merrily every time we ran or stomped past them. Twice a year, on Thanksgiving and Christmas, Nana's Rhine wine glasses were resurrected, as well as the sterling silver water goblets that Mother had collected over the years. The "good" serving ware was used only infrequently, since it was so inconvenient to the kitchen that only an event of some importance justified the effort.

An enormous cut-glass punch bowl, into which family members deposited car keys, mail, and the occasional summons rested on a hulking buffet-hutch. The hutch's shelves and cabinet showcased a motley accumulation of bibelots; the buffet section housed the silver flatware and the table linens, which ranged from the exquisite to the mundane. The buffet was also the repository of the family junk drawer, that staple of every household which serves as a dumping ground for the miscellaneous odd objects that no one knows quite what to do with. Our junk drawer was also the place where rubber bands and old spark plugs went to die when they were no longer hoarded in Paw-Paw's desk.

Our long-time and much-loved cook and housekeeper, Mamie, had left us to spend time in Michigan.

Nana made numerous attempts to replace her, none of them successful for very long. Nana's method of choice for motivating underperforming maids into either shaping up or shipping out was to have them dust and polish the dining-room furniture with its heavily carved, gothic flourishes. The most egregiously ornate of these pieces was the buffet-hutch, and a few maids quit on the spot when confronted with it. We uncharitably referred to this as "the treatment"; all of us cried tears of joy when Mamie returned.

The dining room table seated eighteen with all of its leaves in place. Nana was fond of saying that the table was "as wide as most tables are long." It was lit by an alabaster chandelier whose central dome was surrounded by four globes, giving it the inadvertent look of a trussed turkey. It was not missed after Kevitt demolished it one day while practicing his golf swing.

French doors in the living room opened onto the enclosed side porch, which ran along the Montgomery Street side of the house. It had its own access to the back yard, and shared windows with the dining room, which would otherwise have been deprived of cross-ventilation. With its high ceilings and its surround of tall casement windows, it was especially delightful in the ozone-infused aftermath of summer storms. We learned that this was where Nana, Paw-Paw and their brood retreated during warmer evenings before the installation of the twin six-foot fans at either end of the third floor.

The heat and humidity of a Memphis summer could be pretty oppressive. It was less so inside Poplar Street, with its foot-thick walls, its lofty ceilings and its surrounding shade trees that had matured over the years. The trees cooled the air drawn in by those powerful fans, and lying on the sofa with a good book as the air blew softly through the open windows was pure heaven.

Those breezes died abruptly in the spring of 1952. It was a very warm early June evening, and Daddy decided to oil the fans and get them ready for summer. As it happened, he was a bit oiled himself, and didn't bother to tell anyone what he was about to do before he ascended to the third-floor attic. This turned out to be a serious error. The switch to turn on the attic fan was located below on the second floor, and somebody unknowingly flipped it just as Daddy had his arm and the oil deep inside the blades. Daddy didn't lose his arm, but it took about eighty stitches to close the layers of muscle and skin that had been torn, and shortly thereafter the first of the window air conditioners was installed.

But we still had the side porch.

We could still sit out there after sundown, inhaling the heady scent of honeysuckle, roses and magnolias that drenched the nighttime air.

The porch was furnished with white Victorian wicker chairs, undervalued as usual when they were finally sold. The wicker pieces were interspersed with ugly but functional metal chairs and a hideous vinyl-upholstered metal glider, which Daddy had probably picked up at one of the Beale Street pawn shops when he decided we needed extra seating on the porch.

In the winter, the porch was uninhabitable. Daddy remedied the situation by installing an industrial ceiling heater, so that we could use the space year-round. There was a span of time when we'd erect the Christmas tree there, which made it an attractive spot for the high-school crowd to gather during the Christmas afternoon "open house".

We don't remember whose insane idea it was to move the piano out there, but the instrument suffered badly from the extreme changes in temperature and humidity.

The porch withstood years of wear and tear, including that inflicted by a ferret that Adrienne brought home one day. One of her medical school professors was conducting an experiment utilizing ferrets, and had a few more than he actually required. A friend of Adrienne's had adopted one, but his housemates had rebelled and he needed to find another home for it quickly. Adrienne volunteered to take it off his hands.

The ferret was untamed, untrained, and devoid of redeeming features besides its pretty face. Ferret droppings, known fondly as "sherret fit", littered the porch from one end to the other. Daddy was furious. Then the ferret became ill with distemper and died. Adrienne was allowed to mourn for about ten minutes before Daddy started hounding her to clean the porch, and kept hounding her until the job was completed. It would have taken considerably longer than it did had not Michele and Kevitt, in a rare burst of sympathy, pitched in to help her.

THE LANDSCAPING

Poplar Street's landscape never seemed to be seasonal. It was always there, all the time, or perhaps we didn't notice with our youthful indifference.

The actual landscaping work was figuratively and literally in God's hands, and God did an outstanding job with little help from us. Mother gave it her best effort. When the back lot was converted into our playground, she planted morning glories along the fence that did well until she lost interest. Years later, we would notice hippies staring intently at the morning glories, most likely with the intention of smoking them if they hadn't already.

Mother also put in some rosebushes near the garage, but they suffered from being too close to the spot where one of our sociopathic dogs, Inky, liked to crouch while waiting for somebody to chase to the back porch.

The roses in the front of the house thrived all by themselves. Despite a total lack of pruning or feeding, they continued to yield a profusion of extravagant blooms summer after summer. The jonquils came up every year with no prodding, and the calacanthus, with its pungent, aromatic smell was equally reliable. The magnolia tree continued to reach new heights and to give us its magnificent flowers.

Nana was very protective of the hydrangeas, which produced blossoms that were multihued instead of being the usual red/pink or blue. None of us ever recall seeing her actually tend to them, and we have no idea who planted them or when. There was a small rock garden in the back yard, put there by the original owners. Once, we tried and failed to grow wildflowers in it, but there wasn't enough sun and the soil was too sandy.

Encircling the house was a curious collection of wildly overgrown trees and shrubbery which were, for the most part, self-sufficient. It was a good thing that this was the case, because none of us could grow so much as a wart without killing it.

Uncle Dut and his wife, our Aunt Leeze, were both talented gardeners. Once, they decided to cut back some of that jungle, and spent an entire day beavering away at it. Paw-Paw, who'd never heard of strategic pruning, didn't realize that it was a necessary evil for any thriving yard and refused to believe the reassurances that it would all grow back.

"Not in my lifetime", he grumbled.

Houseplants fared no better, which is why we were taken aback when the nuns at Sacred Heart chose us to care for theirs every summer. When the school year ended, they would deliver their collection to Poplar

Street for safekeeping until they returned in the fall from their motherhouse in Nazareth, Kentucky. One of the nuns, Sister Agathena, entrusted an enormous fern, her pride and joy, to our tender mercies. Kevitt began referring to the plant as "Sister Agathena's Ugh-uh," primarily because it was euphonious; the name, whatever it meant, stuck. We're here to refute the notion that talking to plants helps them. The ones we tended seemed to wither at the sounds of our voices.

For a time, Nana nurtured a cactus. At night, she kept it in the bathtub, where in the dim light it resembled nothing so much as a giant spider. She gave up on it when the younger children's nightmares became problematic. The lilies at Easter and the poinsettias at Christmas all found their ways to the city dump.

So we eventually just grew bored with the whole idea of gardening, and looked forward to visiting our Stonewall Street cousins where we could smell Aunt Leeze's fabulous gardenias.

PERSONAL SPACES

Adrienne and Michele occupied a bedroom, a den and a bath on Poplar Street's third floor. The space was originally intended to be servants' quarters, but had been used as attic storage from the time that Nana and Paw-Paw bought the house. It was accessible via an open back staircase that rose from a hallway on the first floor to end at the third floor landing.

Our sleeping arrangements had become unwieldy. We were sharing a room with five-year-old Kevitt, and relishing making his life miserable. Chris, then two, was still using the crib in Mother's and Daddy's room.

Daddy decided to take action. He used the occasion of Nana's and Paw-Paw's two-week trip to Miami Beach to convert the attic space for our use, so that Chris could be moved in with Kevitt. He first notified a few of his relatives of what he planned to do, which is how Aunt Leeze was able to rescue her wedding dress before it was dispatched to parts unknown. Daddy's next step was to call the Salvation Army and have them back up a truck, into which he unloaded all of the contents of the attic. That these may have included antiques, furnishings, books and papers of some value bothered Daddy not at all, though it bothered his parents quite a bit when they discovered what he'd done.

He also covered the beautiful old hardwood floors with black linoleum tiles which "wouldn't show dirt", using a tarry adhesive that would prove forever impervious to any attempt to remove it.

We immediately took to our new lair. It guaranteed privacy, since none of the grown-ups was interested in making the ascent to our personal belfry, and neither of our brothers was interested in anything we might be doing. The stair treads gratuitously creaked no matter how careful the treader, which served as an effective early-warning system if one of us happened to be entertaining a boyfriend in the den.

The set-up was so perfect that when Adrienne moved permanently to Washington, Michele purred that she would now have the whole third floor to herself. This prompted Chris, still sharing a room with Kevitt, to famously protest that "nobody gets two rooms 'til everybody has one!"

The open stairwell also acted as a megaphone in the days before intercoms and baby monitors, facilitating Daddy's daily wake-up calls. He'd stand at the bottom and roar, "Adrienne! Michele! Rise and shine!" He'd keep at it until he was eventually rewarded with an exasperated, "We're up."

Daddy drove us to school for many years while we were at Sacred Heart. This started after we'd been chastised once too often for failing to show our faces at the morning Mass held daily before school hours even though, as the nuns were fond of phrasing it, we "lived in the shadow of the church!"

We knew that we had to be ready to leave at 7:30, and Daddy knew that we knew, and we all knew that the car was going to leave with us in it. Still, neither of us wanted to dispel Daddy's fantasy that we'd never get up without him to prod us. Even when Michele was older and had moved into an apartment, Daddy would phone her every morning to make sure she'd get to work on time.

Adrienne was especially recalcitrant about getting up when she was in medical school. Mother discovered that the least traumatic way of parting Adrienne from her bed was to allow the smell of toasting pecan Danish dripping with butter to do the job. Mother would then call upstairs, "Adrienne? Your nutty-butty's ready!" Adrienne would be down three flights of stairs, wide-awake, within two minutes.

Kevitt and Chris, who shared one of the front bedrooms on the second floor, were easier meat in the mornings than their older sisters. They tended to get themselves up and organized without too much fanfare—or, at least, Kevitt did. Chris was another matter. He hated going to school.

In first grade, Adrienne, Michele and Kevitt all had a gifted teacher named Sister Ruth Agnes. She loved little children and knew how to motivate them; we still remember her techniques for teaching us how to read.

Unfortunately, she was transferred shortly before Chris was to enter school. Her replacement was a humorless, no-nonsense type who had no patience with the five and six-year-olds under her tutelage.

Chris imitated her to perfection: "Well, if we don't want to do it, we just don't do it, do we?" he'd sing-song whenever any of us showed resistance to doing what we'd been asked to do.

Her stern, forbidding manner literally scared Chris sick. He somehow managed to worry himself into a 100 degree fever on many mornings, and would convince Mother that he was much too ill to go to school.

Mother, helpless in front of the solid evidence on the thermometer, would call the principal's office and notify her that Chris would be absent that day.

Chris would either lie low in his room or mope about the house until early afternoon, when he'd spontaneously recover. Since the school day ended at 2:30, Mother thought it was hardly worth the effort to get him there for the last hour and a half of it. She'd allow him to remain home, and Chris wound up missing forty days of school that year. It was a record. Something in us had to admire the fact that Chris had taken Sister's admonition and turned it on its ear: He didn't want to do it, so he just didn't do it.

For no particular reason, Nana and Paw-Paw would always arise about the same time as the rest of us, though they didn't breakfast until Mamie arrived to cook and serve it. Since they were up, we'd have to vie with them for the use of the washroom off their bedroom, which was very well-lit and much better for applying make-up than our windowless third-floor bathroom with its single overhead bulb.

The second floor bathroom, like Gaul, was divided into three parts. The first section, just off the hallway, housed the shower and a toilet. Since it also served as a pass-through to the next room, one used that toilet only with full awareness that there were no locks on either of the doors.

The middle section was the largest, and held a bathtub, a pedestal sink, and a gas heater which we called the "chill-chaser". Before we had central gas heat, it took awhile after the coal was shoveled into the furnace for the house to warm up. After running through the frigid hallway on a cold morning, plopping on the bath rug to toast in front of the chill-chaser was one of our childhood's great luxuries.

The remaining section of the tripartite bath was a dressing room that augmented Nana's and Paw-Paw's bedroom, which it adjoined. It contained Paw-Paw's closet, a second pedestal sink, and a large built-in storage unit with cabinets above and drawers below that served as a linen closet.

Both the dressing room and the bathtub room had large, east-facing windows that overlooked the corner of Montgomery and Poplar and afforded a broad view of the passing scene. The passing scene was in turn afforded a broad view of us, especially at night when the rooms were lit up in all their glory. The dressing room window had a shade, but at night our backlit silhouettes were plainly visible. This required some gymnastics on our part to avoid providing the locals with a free show.

Running up and down the stairs between our closets and the coveted mirror in the second floor bathroom was only one way we complicated the simple act of getting dressed.

Paw-Paw was fond of a wry saying from his own youth: "First up, best dressed!" For better or for worse, the two of us were able to wear the same clothes. This doubled our wardrobes, but created less incentive to keep everything in wearable condition.

It had been easier when we were younger, because Catholic schools required that everyone wear a uniform. Through eighth grade, girls wore blue jumpers and white blouses. While the blouses were expected to be clean, eventually the jumpers developed a shine that even Johnson's Wax couldn't enhance. In high school, the jumpers gave way to skirts and blazers, and these were deemed acceptable as long as they didn't exhibit what we had for lunch.

The nuns always encouraged us to "walk proudly," because the uniforms, whatever their condition, indicated to students in other schools that we were good Catholics. What the nuns couldn't fathom was that students in other schools couldn't have cared less if we'd been Druids. What they were probably thinking, watching us saunter past them on our way home, was what twits we were, wearing twitty uniforms at that.

Once into college and out of our uniforms, the clothes situation quickly deteriorated. Not to put too fine a point on it, but we were slobs. Skirts, blouses, sweaters and dresses in varying states of cleanliness were strewn with abandon all over our rooms. Mother would sometimes give in and launder a few things, but for the most part we just waded through the rubble until we found something that was more or less presentable.

In that era, everyone wore white socks. When our supply dwindled to a critical level, Michele's insurance policy was to wear a pair to bed to make sure she'd have some in the morning.

Adrienne was undeterred. If she was in too big of a hurry to excavate her own socks from the communal heap in the middle of the floor, she'd simply steal over to Michele's bed, gently lift the covers from her sister's feet, and slide the socks off them. Michele, the soundest sleeper this side of the morgue, would never even stir.

Being assured of something to wear became especially important to Michele when Adrienne was required to be on call for autopsies, which was the first step in conditioning future doctors to be alert for emergencies at any time. The medical students had to be available on a rotating basis to assist at these procedures, ideally conducted as soon as possible after death. Since people don't always die between nine and five, the University of Tennessee medical student could count on having to hightail it over to John Gaston Hospital at 2 or 3 a.m. at least once during the months then devoted to the study of pathology.

The problem was that a 3 a.m. autopsy might not be finished until about 7:30 a.m. Adrienne would race home in time to throw on some fresh clothes and then make it back to the medical center for an 8:00 a.m. class.

Michele was in college at the time, and was scheduled one day to make a presentation in an English class. Knowing that she would be judged on her appearance as well as on her content, she dutifully cleaned up a little green suit, carefully ironing it and accessorizing it.

In the back of her head, though, she knew what was going to happen. Adrienne would get a middle-of-the-night call to the hospital and return home with no time to spare. She'd then change into the first thing she saw in the closet and race out again. Michele knew the little green suit could be a casualty, and since she couldn't wear *it* to bed, decided to appeal to Adrienne's better nature.

She wrote a note and spiked it through the hanger. The note read: "Please do not wear me. Michele has spent a long time washing and ironing me so she'll look good in her English class today where she has to make a presentation. Love, The Little Green Suit."

Sure enough, Michele's premonition was accurate. Adrienne got home just as the dawn was breaking and flew up the steps. Michele slept through whatever happened next. But when she arose, the suit was gone and a new note appeared on the empty hanger:

"Help! I've been kidnapped!

(signed) The Little Green Suit."

In a parallel universe, Michele would have put the suit between the mattress and the box springs and slept well, knowing that it was safe. But Poplar Street, while certainly a contender as a parallel universe, dealt primarily with physical reality in its observation of the First-Up-Best-Dressed rule.

THE BASEMENT

Poplar Street's dark, dim basement was frightening to us when we were small, and we placed it in the same sinister category as Aunt Lizzie's house on McNeil. Getting down to it required navigating a rickety wooden staircase which was devoid of handrails and which threatened to momentarily collapse. It led to a concrete-floored room dominated by the huge furnace, ducts sprouting from it to creep along the low ceiling. It looked like a large metal Medusa glinting in what little light penetrated the one filthy window.

When the furnace was coal-fired, Paw-Paw would tend it. Getting invited to help him was exciting, since we got to pick up pieces of coal and throw them onto the glowing embers.

Adjacent to the furnace room was a second room where the coal was stored. A small hinged window near its ceiling opened to admit the chute through which the coal was delivered.

We didn't know what lay behind the furnace and didn't want to know. Rumor had it that somewhere in the basement was the still that the family had used to ensure the flow of alcohol during Prohibition. The most likely hiding place for that particular piece of equipment would have been in Paw-Paw's wine cellar, accessible through a heavy door on the south side of the furnace room. If it was kept there, it would not have been recognizable under its thick blanket of dust.

We shuddered at the thought of what creatures might lurk in the gloomy depths of the basement. The cobwebs that shrouded every nook and cranny denoted a thriving spider population, and the occasional large beetle would creep into view.

Mice remained a perennial problem as they commuted between the basement and the kitchen. Each night, Paw-Paw would go into the kitchen and set out mousetraps baited with whatever cheese was on sale at Kroger's. Within five minutes of the lights being extinguished, a rapid-fire series of thwacks would signal that another half-dozen mice had received their wings.

Poplar Street's varmints were not confined to the basement and the kitchen, however. There was a whole army of miscellaneous critters that lived behind the walls, unseen by us but not unheard. The spaces around and above our rooms on the third floor teemed with them, and all night long bats and squirrels would frolic about, racing above our ceilings from one side of the house to the other. After awhile, the sounds of their squeaking, brushing, swishing and thudding blended with noises of the street traffic outside to become a lullaby. As adults, it took us awhile to learn to fall asleep with silence.

There was an unusual trap door built into the wall of our bedroom closet. We always regarded it with some trepidation, but felt it was good to diversify our terrors and so never bothered to see where it led.

With the advent of gas heat and the departure of the coal, the basement was utilized more and so lost its nether-worldly mystique. Daddy and our Uncle Marine Rowe put in a train set for Kevitt. Later, a washing machine and dryer were installed. Later still, Mother's kiln, where she fired her ceramics, made its appearance.

THE BASEMENT AND THE BOMB

The USSR's detonation of its first atomic bomb sent the nation into a collective tizzy over the possibility of a nuclear attack. Everywhere, people were either constructing backyard bomb shelters or tricking out their basements to conform to the recommendations of the Civil Defense Administration.

Adrienne scared herself witless at the age of ten when she read and essentially memorized a tome entitled *You Can Survive An Atomic Bomb.* She knew just how many roentgens were necessary to produce which dreadful symptoms of radiation poisoning. She'd calculated that the corner of Cleveland and Madison represented Ground Zero, and knew what the blast, heat and radiation effects of a one- kiloton bomb dropped at that location would be at various distances away from it.

The United States conducted nuclear tests at Yucca Flats, New Mexico. Adrienne and Mimi were sledding down the hills at Tech High one day following a snowstorm, when they were called back to the house. There'd been a report that the snow was radioactive, because fallout from the New Mexico tests had drifted over Memphis.

At Poplar Street, we were told to go to the basement wine cellar in the event we were attacked. Michele never thought that was prudent, and told Daddy that if a bomb dropped the whole house would come crashing down on us. Daddy pointed out that the foundation pillars that held up the house would continue to do so, and that we'd be safe. Adrienne suggested that we adopt Mother's plane crash precautions and line up some beds, crawl under them, and trust that the house would bounce off the mattresses.

Our elders' evasiveness when pressed about these matters was not reassuring. Daddy seemed to dodge the question of how we were supposed to get out once the radioactivity and the firestorms had diminished. We also wondered what we'd eat, since there were no provisions stocked and nobody seemed inclined to go out and buy any. We assumed that we would live on wine and whiskey until we were either rescued or went to that Happy Hour in the sky.

The nuns at school put their own spin on this frenzied state of affairs. They missed no opportunity to impress upon us that the godless Communists could bomb us at any time, so it was important to keep our immortal souls in a state of grace. And, of course, we should pray for courage because the Communists would naturally kill anyone who was Catholic, and we had to be prepared to die for our faith. We knew we were sitting ducks because of our uniforms, which announced to the world that we attended a Catholic school. The Russians would know exactly which ones to kill, we thought. We might not even get a chance for one last Hail Mary.

The nuns would beam with the pride of a mission accomplished as we would sit at lunch time in the cafeteria eating our tuna sandwiches and anxiously discussing the Book of Revelations, the world coming to an end in 1960, and the Third Secret of Fatima. The latter supposedly contained a prophecy so horrendous that the Pope, upon reading it, was said to have swooned.

Every Saturday at noon, the air raid siren would go off in Memphis as a "practice" drill in case Armageddon came. We wondered if we were the only ones who realized that if the Russians were serious about destroying Memphis, the ideal time to do it would be: at noon on a Saturday. We weren't quite sure why Memphis would be considered a prime target in the first place, unless somebody in the Kremlin had an axe to grind with either the Cotton Exchange or Elvis. But there were still those of us who said a prayer of thanks when the air raid drill was over and we discovered we hadn't yet been vaporized.

The Russian Attack Scenario prompted our first real all-out effort to worry the last drop out of something in hopes that God would decide we'd suffered enough and spare us. The practice has served us well through the years in that we're still alive as this is written, though we substitute "Iran", "Al Qaeda," and "rogue nation" for Russia.

PETS

The term "pets" is used here loosely, to denote members of different species who happened to inhabit the premises with us from time to time. They were by no means the highly esteemed members of the family that so many pets are today.

The only animal that came close to achieving this status—though still missing it by a country mile—was Ching, a Pekingese given to us by one of Kevitt's and Chris's doctors. The reason why Mother agreed to take the dog is lost to history. Her disgruntlement about having to care for the animals that everyone else ignored after the honeymoon was over was well-known, so we were somewhat mystified when Ching appeared on the scene.

CHING

Ching got our attention by biting Nana during his first five minutes in residence. We'd learned by painful experience how easily an animal could be threatened by all of us descending upon it at once, and this knowledge made us give Ching a bit more space than we might have otherwise. It didn't much matter.

We remained evenly divided as to whether Ching was psychotic or merely eccentric.

He did have his quirks. His bark sounded like the cry of a colicky infant, which was disconcerting.

He was mortally afraid of thunderstorms, and took two approaches, depending upon whether the household was awake or asleep. At night, he would go streaking up the back stairs, his shrieks reverberating through the house, until he reached our room on the third floor and scooted to safety under Michele's bed. During daylight hours, he diverted to the second floor bathroom and launched himself into the old claw-foot tub, where he continued to wail inconsolably until the storm passed. Daddy had read somewhere that the bathtub was the safest place to be during a thunderstorm, and believed that Ching's recognition of this was a mark of his high intelligence. But then, Daddy also thought that people who could spread their toes wouldn't get cancer.

Ching had a preference for dark, close environments, and spent a fair amount of time burrowed under the cushions of the overupholstered chairs and sofas in Poplar Street's living room. Unsuspecting visitors who innocently sat down would have the bejesus scared out of them when the cushions beneath them erupted in squeals and heaves.

It was Ching who ratted Adrienne out when she started smoking at the age of fourteen. She had a beanbag ashtray that she kept under her bed, and one day Mother had come upstairs and the two of them were talking. At some point in the conversation, Ching showed up and began snuffling around under the bed. Before Adrienne could stop him, he'd nosed the ashtray, brimming with butts and trailing ashes, out into view. Mother stared at it, speechless. Caught red-handed, the only thing Adrienne could offer was a weak, "My friends smoke a lot?"

One of our neighbors had a female Pekingese, and contacted Daddy about breeding her to Ching. Daddy was bursting with pride. Someone else had realized what a fine specimen of canine perfection he had in this marvelous dog! A wedding date was set.

However, when the big day arrived, Ching disdained his bride and adamantly refused her favors. Daddy felt Ching's manhood had been impugned, and he said that well, he didn't blame Ching a bit, that he wouldn't have had anything to do with her either, after all, she had DILBERRIES! This marked the only time in the history of creation that a male dog refused to mate with a female because of her lack of proper hygiene.

We never knew what happened to Ching, because one day he just vanished. He loved riding in cars, and if a car door opened while he was outdoors he'd be through it in a heartbeat. Since our house was on a busy corner and situated between two schools, there were many cars being parked in close proximity to us. We theorized that somebody opened a car door and didn't notice that Ching had gained entry. We thought that maybe by the time the driver realized he had a passenger, it was too late to figure out when or where he'd come on board, and the driver just kept him.

We spent a month searching for him, even putting an ad in the newspaper. There were several leads, but none of them panned out. Finally, all we could do was hope that Ching had landed in a good spot.

TAM

Adrienne's earliest animal memories are of Tam, who held the dubious honor of Family Pet when she was born. Officially christened Tam O'Shanter, Tam was a Scottish Terrier who had nothing but scorn for everyone except Paw-Paw, to whom he was devoted. In fairness to Tam, he was not a young dog when the first of the grandchildren came bothering him. His MO was to crawl under the huge Victorian buffet in the dining room, from which vantage point he'd growl and snarl at any toddler making its precarious way toward him. Mimi, who was braver than the rest of us, found out the hard way that he wasn't bluffing. Fortunately, the bite wasn't a bad one, though the ensuing uproar took a ribbon or two.

Within the family, Tam was regarded as being vastly superior to Gaga, his litter-mate. Gaga lived with Paw-Paw's brother and two sisters in their mausoleum of a house on McNeil Street. The only light in their living room streamed from an old Tiffany chandelier, which cast a forbidding glow on the furniture's heavily carved wood but mercifully lacked the wattage to reveal Gaga's handiwork on the velvet drapes and the upholstery. Compared with Gaga, Tam was a prince among men.

Tam died of old age around 1949. Naturally, we weren't told that he was dying; just that he was "going to the farm", where he'd get better.

At no time do we ever recall a veterinarian getting into the act when any of our "pets" became sick. A trip to the farm was the standard remedy for a life-threatening illness. From the standpoint of our elders, it was idiot-proof: 1) the animal could be said to remain there for as long as it took for us to quit asking about it, on the accurate assumption that we'd eventually get bored with hearing the same vague answers; and 2) they wouldn't have to put up with all the weeping and gnashing of teeth, not to mention the tiresome discussions about dog heaven, that would undoubtedly follow if we knew the truth.

YIPPEE

The Farm was not involved in Yippee's swan song. Yippee was a beautiful but totally deranged Collie who was in and out of the house during Tam's tenure, though we saw considerably less of him than we did of Tam. No one remembers how he came to join the household, but we suspect that he just showed up in the yard one day and the alcoholic maid we had at the time gave him a bowl of beer.

Yippee's claim to fame was his Houdini-like ability to escape any bonds with which he was tethered.

A fierce battle of wills ensued between Yippee and Paw-Paw, which Yippee inevitably won. Every night, Paw-Paw would announce that Yippee couldn't possibly get loose THIS time, and every morning we'd get the usual calls from outraged neighbors claiming that Yippee'd either raided their garbage can, raped their dog, dug up their garden or bitten their kid. We were very lucky that people hadn't yet been trained to reflexively sue each other over every little aggravation.

Paw-Paw finally decided to lock Yippee in the room in the basement where we stored the coal for the furnace, the room being almost empty at the time. At the top of the room was a paned window, which could be opened to provide access for the coal delivery truck's chute. The next morning, one of the window's six-inch panes was broken and Yippee was gone—permanently, as it turned out. Someone darkly suggested that he was possessed, and that Satan had claimed his own.

INKY

Only Daddy could have thought that an abused dog would make a good family pet. One afternoon, he walked in the door carrying a small black Cocker Spaniel. He announced that it had belonged to a boy who stuck pencils in its ears, and that the boy's father had given the dog, whose name was Inky, to us. And wasn't that wonderful?

Things did not get off to a good start. Daddy, who couldn't wait to show off his latest acquisition, invited the extended family over for a look-see and a few drinks. The poor dog, suspicious of human contact from the get-go, was subjected to the excited ministrations of all of us kids instead of being allowed to adjust to his new surroundings at his own pace. As time passed, his skittishness only worsened, and eventually he snapped so much that Daddy put him on a dog run which extended from the house to the garage. He unclipped Inky from it only at night, releasing him to sleep on the back porch.

Inky remained vigilant for any opportunity to attack one of us. Despite having attained the girth of a barrel, he was surprisingly fast on his feet. He knew that we'd have to cross his path to get from the car to the house, and would lie in wait, lurking in the bushes next to the garage where his obsidian fur would merge with the shadows. When he'd suddenly materialize, we'd make a mad dash for the porch, trying to get there before Inky did. On the positive side, any one of us could have excelled at track.

Occasionally, there'd be a slip-up; somebody would leave the back door ajar, and Inky would rush inside. The cry would go up: "INKY'S IN THE HOUSE!!" We'd all run for safety—up the stairs, atop the dining room table, out the front door. After a spirited chase around the house, one of the grown-ups would collar him, drag him back outside, and sound the all-clear.

One spring day, Grandpa Weber, Mother's father, came over. He disapproved of the fact that the back yard, Inky's domain, was barren of any plant life, and was determined that peonies should grow there. It took him most of the day to dig at least a dozen foot-deep holes, plant the bulbs, and fill in the dirt. Unfortunately, Grandpa failed to consider that peonies do not thrive when fed a steady diet of dog urine, which Inky provided in copious quantities as soon as they started to sprout. Not a one survived, and that was the end of the beautification efforts.

Inky's departure for The Farm was without fanfare.

SNAPPY AND HAPPY AND SPEEDO THE DUCK

In the days before the animal rights activists declared that animals were people, too, the coming of Easter meant that Woolworth's five-and-dime was selling baby chicks dyed in pastel tints. One Good Friday, Mother arrived home with two of them, purchased on a whim. She presented them to Kevitt and Chris, who named the lavender one Snappy and the blue one Happy.

None of us expected the chicks to last the night, much less until Easter Sunday. However, Mamie, our wise and wonderful maid, knew a few things about raising chickens. Thanks to her expertise, our brothers managed to keep Snappy and Happy on this side of the daisies. They set up a makeshift incubator in the kitchen, where they danced constant attendance under Mamie's tutelage.

It didn't take long for Snappy and Happy to outgrow the cardboard box and graduate to a cage on the side porch. It didn't take long after that for them to outgrow the cage and graduate to the back lot, where we had our swings and our sandbox. And it didn't take long after that for Snappy and Happy to become very large and very territorial roosters.

The instant the gate was opened, the two would come flying at the intruder, hissing loudly with wings flapping and beaks thrusting. They even had a tag-team play down pat which they employed if more than one person invaded their bailiwick. Anyone who made it as far as one of the swings knew to stand on it and get airborne as quickly as possible, since the roosters were undaunted by their frequent collisions with the swing as they dive-bombed it.

The only person who could get near them was Clara, who rented the apartment above the garage and whose speech bore a strong resemblance to the cluck of a hen. We marveled at the sight of Snappy and Happy literally eating out of Clara's hand, with the three of them chattering away at each other in chickenspeak.

However, the roosters had become so adept at military maneuvers that it became impossible for us to use our playground.

Meanwhile, Uncle Dut and Aunt Leeze had made an Easter gift of Speedo the Duck to their children: Marilou, Sherry and Justin. He was a tiny little thing, all yellow and downy, and looked as though he'd just stepped from a Peeps box. We thought he was adorable.

He didn't stay that way. As with Snappy and Happy, Speedo's growth spurt was not a positive development.

It seemed that Speedo's gastrointestinal tract was in a state of perpetual motion, resulting in his banishment to the outdoors. Pretty soon, our cousins couldn't use their swings or sandbox, either, because their entire back yard was Speedo's latrine.

When Aunt Leeze caught her toddler Justin sampling Speedo's droppings, the handwriting was on the wall. Uncle Dut called Daddy: Speedo was going to The Farm, and would Snappy and Happy care to join him? Daddy responded that they would indeed, but allowed as to how he was going to need some help catching them.

Uncle Dut arrived within the hour with Aunt Leeze and our cousins in tow and a now-defunct Speedo in the trunk. The party line was that Speedo was "taking a nap, so he'll be ready to play when he gets to The Farm!"

The women and children all clustered outside the fence to watch the show, and Daddy and Uncle Dut opened the gate. Snappy and Happy made to attack, but when Daddy lunged at one of them they realized that this wasn't going to be the usual walk in the park. Reconnoitering swiftly, they took off and half-ran, half-flew in the other direction. Considering their ages and the amount of bourbon Daddy'd had before dinner, Daddy and Uncle Dut displayed a fair amount of agility as they charged after the roosters, faking right and running left in full high-school football mode.

Then, touchdown! Daddy tackled Snappy. He threw Snappy to the ground and quickly tied his feet with a piece of rope. Flush with triumph, Daddy stood up and turned to the wildly applauding peanut gallery, completely unaware that Snappy had righted himself. With feet still bound, Snappy hopped purposefully over to where Daddy was taking a deep ceremonial bow and bit him square on the butt.

There was a moment of stunned silence before we all burst into hysterical laughter.

We'd heard Daddy cuss before, but the string of profanity that erupted from him at that moment pretty much retired the jersey. When Uncle Dut caught Happy, it was anticlimactic. It also dispelled any delusions that any of us might still be harboring about The Farm.

JUDAS AND THE PIGEONS

All the birds we tried to keep managed to escape. The ceilings of Poplar Street were high, and the bird merely had to wait for cage-cleaning time to make a run for it. They all learned that if they kept flying from the top of one drapery rod to another, their pursuers would eventually tire of moving the ladder around and go away. From there, it became a simple matter to find an open door or window and get airborne.

Judas was a finch who lasted longer than most—at least long enough to give Michele psittacosis pericarditis. Adrienne had bought him as a present for a sorority sister, who essentially refused delivery. So Adrienne brought it home, where it was ensconced in the third floor den where the ceilings were lower. Adrienne had carelessly situated its cage over the heating vent, with the result that Judas thought it was June and molted. By the time we realized what was happening, the bird was bald and Michele was getting sick.

It took awhile for the doctors to figure out what was ailing her. This was to be expected. She's never been easy to diagnose, since a pain in her knee could easily signify an ear infection. But figure it out they did, probably aided by the fact that Memphis had a large pigeon population. These pigeons harbored a fair amount of both psittacosis and histoplasmosis, diseases which kept the city's internal medicine specialists in business and on their toes. Though we couldn't be sure whether it was Judas or the pigeons that infected Michele, suffice it to say that Judas was given his freedom. Michele achieved celebrity status as being one of only 50 cases in the country that year of pericarditis directly attributable to psittacosis.

There's an old joke about life that says, "Some days you're the pigeon, and some days you're the statue." At Poplar Street, you were a statue every day. There was a large family of pigeons that regarded our eaves as their private breeding ground. Their sheer numbers injected an element of double jeopardy when we raced Inky for the porch. In addition to evading Inky, we also had to dodge the pigeon poop that would suddenly drop from above the back door, or that would hit us via sniper fire from the squadrons of pigeons in flight. Members of the family frequently held newspapers over their heads as they left the house to avoid having their finery ruined, which had happened several times.

Or not: Nana was wearing her new beige spring coat to church one Sunday morning. The back of it featured a tone-on-tone embroidered design consisting of rayed lines fanning out from a central triangle. Seeing her walking toward the car, Paw-Paw honestly thought a bird had scored on it. Nana was indignant. She went back inside and changed, and the next day returned the coat to the store for a refund.

There were so many pigeons that Daddy would periodically corral all of us into the house, get out his firearm of choice and proceed to thin the herd. He'd always warn Clara to stay in her apartment until the shooting stopped, after which she'd collect the corpses and boil them up in a large cauldron. Watching her stir the smelly brew over an open fire in the back yard brought to mind images better suited to Halloween than a spring evening.

For years, Daddy used a BB gun for this operation, spring-loaded so that it made little noise when fired. Later, he upgraded to a 22 caliber rifle loaded with birdshot which was loud enough that it occasionally attracted the attention of the local constabulary. Kevitt learned to keep an eye out for police cruisers patrolling around the house when a pigeon extermination was in progress.

Daddy's attempts to eradicate Poplar Street's birds, beasts and bugs did not always end well. Once, in an

effort to remove a wasps' nest next to his second floor
bedroom window, he stood on the ground with a hose
and aimed the water directly at the nest. Several enter-
prising wasps flew straight down the stream of water
and stung Daddy unmercifully on the hand. Shortly
after that, Poplar Street was added to Orkin Pest Control's customer base.

BOOSHAY

Clara doted upon her yappy little dog, Booshay,
whose small, hairless face gave evidence that a Chihua-
hua bloomed somewhere on his multi-branched family
tree. He had the distinction of being probably the only
animal to reside at Poplar Street who was actually a
beloved pet. We never could figure out if Booshay was
actually his name, or whether it was Clara's way of pro-
nouncing something else. Whatever the case, when we
called "Booshay!" he'd come running.

Booshay also had the distinction of being the
only sentient being ever to befriend Inky. He'd
keep Inky company while the latter skulked around
the foliage awaiting the opportunity to ambush
somebody.

However, we remember him chiefly because Nana
immortalized him in a song she made up to amuse
Kevitt when he was small. The lyrics consisted of nam-
ing all the people and animals who would "go by",
and Kevitt's hands-down favorite verse led off with
"Booshay go by!"

HERE BOY

Here Boy was a scrawny, defeated-looking cur whom Mother adopted. He never made it inside the house, but every day Mother would go into the yard calling, "Here, boy! Here, boy!" He'd crawl out from wherever he'd slumped, and Mother would feed him. Needless to say, Here Boy responded to her care, and started to perk up. Flesh began to cover his bones, his coat appeared healthier, and he started to project an aura of well-being. Then, one day, Here Boy showed up with a WOMAN in tow. Mother took an instant dislike to her. The female bullied Here Boy, pushing him out of the way and eating all of the food Mother had set out. After this happened several times, Mother gave up and left Here Boy to learn about the finer things of life from his concubine, who apparently had found greener pastures for Here Boy and herself.

MING TOY

Given the semi-positive experience we'd had earlier with Ching, our family naturally rushed to the judgment that a Pekingese was the best possible dog that anyone could own. Ming Toy was the last of Poplar Street's misbegotten menagerie, a deformed Peke that Michele discovered pining away in a local pet shop. He was well past the bloom of puppyhood, and Michele took one look at his asymmetrically bulging eyes, realized he was slated for extinction, and decided he'd make the perfect Father's Day present.

Daddy and Ming were well-matched, since neither of them was much constrained by the bounds of propriety. Presumably to avoid breaking Ming's spirit, Daddy allowed him to remain in his pristinely untrained state. The dog's "official" bathroom was the newspaper-bedecked downstairs back hallway, which was enclosed when the doors were shut and which also served as his nighttime habitat. His "unofficial" bathroom could be anywhere he pleased, and, to Daddy's delight, ON anybody he pleased.

Ming was confined to the kitchen during the day, but alert for any chance to broaden his horizons. If somebody left a door open, he would charge into the dining room, marking his territory as he went, with Daddy in gleeful pursuit.

By the time Michele acquired him, Ming already answered to his name. When we found out later that Ming Toy meant "Daughter of Happiness", we decided that his inclination toward interspecies mating may have inspired it.

Daddy was quite proud of his success in teaching Ming to dance, and viewed this as an indication of Ming's superior breeding. The little dog would frenetically hop around on his two strong hind legs, hoping against hope that he'd get a milk bone out of the deal.

Ming's services as a watch dog were limited. One Sunday, while Mother and Daddy were at church, someone broke into the house. The burglar had hurled a rock through one of the back door's glass panes, made it to the second floor, and stolen Daddy's gun. When our parents returned, they immediately saw the damage to the door and the rock that had inflicted it. Ming had apparently welcomed the intruder with both open paws and an open bladder, as the rock lying on the kitchen floor was still wet from its recent baptism.

After Daddy's death, Mother refused to put up with Ming's antics any longer. She gave him to her sister, Aunt Mary Frances, another iconoclast and probably the only other person on the planet besides our father who actually liked Ming. However, when Aunt Mary decided at age seventy to get married for the first time to one of her old boyfriends and move to Florida, Ming was quickly deemed expendable. She palmed him off on one of her neighbors, who knew Ming's ways and didn't mind adopting an elderly dog. We presume they lived happily ever after.

BULL

Bull, short for Bullshit, was the name Kevitt gave to a stray cat that he'd rescued from certain death. Bull had to remain in the wild, so to speak, since Nana loathed cats and refused to be anywhere near one.

When Adrienne was eighteen, she had a front-row seat at Nana's last and most definitive encounter with a cat. The two of them were visiting Chicago, staying with Nana's niece, Mary Jane. Mary Jane had joined a Carmelite convent, but before taking her final vows she decided that this was not the life for her and had very recently left the order. This meant making a transition back into the modern world from that of a medieval monastery, where total silence had been observed and the dining table had featured a skull for a centerpiece. It couldn't have been easy for her, and having guests under foot was probably an added stress.

Sharing the house were two other people and Mary Jane's cat, which was suffering from some unsightly skin disease and was missing large clumps of fur as a result. Mary Jane was quite attached to the cat, and allowed it to jump onto the table during dinner. Nana could barely contain herself.

Adrienne, recognizing impending disaster when she saw it, called everyone she knew in Chicago in an effort to spend as much time as possible elsewhere. Within an hour, she was booked solid.

Several nights into their visit, she came in from a date to find Nana pacing the floor in high dudgeon.

"Call the Hilton!" Nana commanded Adrienne. She was so angry that her voice shook. "I'm not spending one more minute in this lunatic asylum!"

"What happened?"

"THAT HELLISH CAT ATTACKED ME!"

Nana had been soundly sleeping, unaware that she was occupying Mary Jane's bed and equally unaware that the cat slept there, too. The cat, miffed at being booted from its place of honor and determined to reclaim it, took a flying leap and landed on Nana, who awakened screaming in terror.

Since it was obvious that Nana was adamant about leaving, it was a good thing that fortune smiled in the form of a respectable hotel that would permit a three a.m. check-in. Adrienne and Nana departed Mary Jane's with the most perfunctory of good-byes, and Nana never occupied the same house with a cat again as long as she lived.

So Bull, for reasons of necessity, was an outside cat. He was allowed access to the back porch, where his favorite spot was the top rung of the eight-foot ladder. One Sunday, Uncle Dut et.al. arrived for our ritual dinner, with Sherry carrying her miniature poodle. Bull, viewing this opportunity from his vantage point, couldn't resist. He sprang down, sinking his claws into the poodle. Sherry was distraught, the poodle was frantic, and Bull was almost history.

Eventually, somebody came across Bull giving birth to a litter of kittens, which was the first inkling anyone had that Bull was actually a cow. Kevitt named one of the surviving kittens Minotaur, meaning "son of bull". Minotaur was the first in a long line of Bullshette's feral descendants who no doubt plague Poplar Street— and maybe even all of Memphis—to this day.

POPLAR STREET VISITORS

It was always a crapshoot as to who else was going to be joining us on Poplar Street at any given time. Friends, relatives, perfect strangers—who knew? It added an element of suspenseful excitement to getting up in the morning.

Sometimes, we'd get uninvited guests. Down the street from us was a private psychiatric clinic, where supervision of the patients was occasionally somewhat lax. One morning, Adrienne stumbled, half-asleep, down the back stairs and into the kitchen, drawn by the aroma of brewing coffee. She was startled into wakefulness by the sight of an unfamiliar woman slumped in one of the chairs, hair in disarray and clad in a bathrobe and slippers. The woman had apparently eluded her captors at the clinic, wandered down Poplar, and let herself into the house via the unlocked front door. She was carrying on a disjointed conversation with Nana, who was trying to humor her while a visibly annoyed Paw-Paw contacted the clinic to have someone come and fetch her.

The clinic was a thorn in the family side. The proprietor, a psychiatrist, had emigrated from Germany and had somehow landed in Memphis. The problem was that he'd legally changed his name to one that was very similar to Uncle Dut's, and his clinic was on Poplar. The result was that both our households had to field calls intended either for the good shrink or for his facility, which was irksome given that the callers were not always in contact with reality. Finding the random clinic escapee on our hands further strained the relationship with our neighbor.

However, the vast majority of our visitors were there by invitation from at least one of us, not that this carried with it any imperative to inform anyone else that company was coming.

Nana's brothers Uncle Non and Uncle Duddy would each come down to spend a few days with us every now and then when both were residing in Chicago. We children were rarely given more than a day's notice of their impending arrival, because we would invariably be ordered to play musical beds and the grown-ups didn't care to listen to our resentful muttering any longer than was absolutely necessary. One time, the first we knew that Uncle Duddy was visiting was when we saw him sitting in the living room. Spotting him, Adrienne announced firmly that she wasn't giving up HER bed, and that it was somebody else's turn. Daddy and Nana gasped in horror at this gross breach of etiquette, but Adrienne did get to sleep in her own bed that night.

A third brother of Nana's, Uncle Bill, would sometimes come with his wife, Aunt Annie. In the hot summer of 1946, Adrienne, Michele and Mimi had stayed with them at their home in East St. Louis, where we were introduced to the joys of running through the lawn sprinkler clad only in our underpants.

Their trips to Memphis were a treat for us. We looked forward to seeing them and to seeing their daughters, Ann and Connie. Ann was the widow of Bill Engelhart, and Michele was enamored of their son, Billy, who was twenty at the time of one of their visits. Michele, who was three, had flirted shamelessly with Billy all afternoon, but when he was leaving, she went behind the sofa and adamantly refused to come out to kiss everyone good-bye. It turned out that she'd been having much too good a time to waste any of it on a bathroom break, and disaster had struck— resulting in what passes for embarrassment if you're only three years old.

While Billy Engelhart had the distinction of being the first inappropriate male object of Michele's affections, the second was Oscar, the foreman of the crew that Daddy hired to repaint the downstairs walls not long after the Engelharts called on us. Though not technically a visitor, Oscar did endear himself, especially to Michele.

While Michele's crush on Charming Billy was understandable, her crush on Oscar was not. Oscar brought to mind Ichabod Crane, with his tall, gangly frame. He had woefully bad skin, and his smile revealed a mouth dominated by a large gold tooth that hung down on one side, which he used primarily to anchor the stogie that he smoked incessantly. His two redeeming features were his booming, infectious laugh and his soft spot for little Michele.

She would follow him with her paper and crayons to wherever he was painting. She'd spend most of the day drawing pictures of him, presenting each new artwork to him for his enthusiastic approval. While he painted and she drew, the two of them would carry on extended conversations.

One day, Michele was outdoors playing and on impulse decided to climb the magnolia tree. Higher and higher she ascended, and when she finally stopped climbing she was about forty feet off the ground. Terrified, she began to scream. Mother ran outside, saw what had happened and cried out for help. Oscar was there almost before the echo of her screams died. He climbed up the tree, caught Michele, and brought her back down to safety, achieving hero status immediately in Michele's eyes.

We mention this story to dispute the family conventional wisdom that Michele never married because she was too picky.

THE SUMMER VISITORS AND RAINBOW LAKE

The highlight of any of our summers was a visit by our out-of-town cousins.

Uncle Jack and his wife, our Aunt Cassie, would travel from Washington, D.C. with their four children.

John was the oldest, and the first of Nana's and Paw-Paw's grandchildren. Next was Jim, who was the same age as Adrienne, Marilou and Mimi. Cassie Beth, their older daughter, was next in line among the cousins chronologically, followed by Michele, Bill, and Sherry. Trish, the youngest, was a contemporary of Kevitt and Carol Rowe.

Aunt Ding and her family would drive up to Memphis from their home in Dallas. Her daughters, Ann and Missy, bridged the age gap between the first and second wave of female cousins. Her son Walter, called Sonny, was Kevitt's, Carol's and Trish's age.

All of the Memphis cousins were very fond of the Dallas and Washington branches of the family. When they were five years old, Adrienne and Marilou would argue over who was going to get to marry John.

These summer visits were always occasions for picnics at Rainbow Lake, which was a public complex that included a swimming pool, picnic grounds with tables and barbecue grills set in stone foundations, a pavilion with a juke box, and an indoor ballroom which was the scene of numerous dances and receptions that we attended when we were older.

Once, we had a family picnic at Clearpool, another pool-picnic facility farther out Lamar Avenue, but this departure from the norm was a one-time thing. Unlike the pool at Rainbow Lake, the one at Clearpool was round, with the deepest part in the middle, and the water was always unpleasantly frigid.

At other times, we went to Clearpool only when Rainbow Lake was overcrowded. When we did, Mother consistently impressed us with her racing dive into what couldn't have been more than two feet or so of water. She'd been an expert swimmer, an accomplishment which neither of her daughters would ever come close to matching. It took Adrienne four years to learn to swim, with three of those years spent clutching the side of the pool in abject terror.

We were much too excited to sleep for long on the day of a picnic. We would awaken to the redolent smells of chicken frying in lard and of the breakfast that awaited us. Ham with milk gravy, homemade biscuits and fruit would be set out in the dining room, and we'd make quick work of it. Then, we'd pile into the car and accompany Daddy to the ice house. There, he'd purchase both a large block of ice and several bags of the chipped variety. The latter was used to fill the nooks and crannies of the coolers where the beer, soft drinks and perishable foods would be chilled.

Going to the ice house was always considered a treat, as it provided a welcome relief from the intense heat of Memphis summers in the days before air-conditioning. When the door to the loading dock was opened, we'd stand in front of it and quiver with pleasure as the blast of chilled air washed over us.

Family lore has it that one time during World War II, Daddy had iced down a case of beer in one of the coolers. Things had apparently gotten off to a late start, and when Daddy lifted the cooler it felt suspiciously light. The maid at the time, around whom no bottle of vanilla was safe, had drunk up half the beer. Everyone but Daddy was incensed. Daddy, unfazed, just added another bottle of bourbon to the picnic provisions. He'd never been much of a beer drinker anyway, even though the beer that he'd made during Prohibition had been in great demand among his friends and/or whoever had the cash to pay for it.

The extended family would gather at Poplar Street, and all the food, drink, bathing suits, towels, plates, utensils, charcoal, toys, strollers, infant cribs and children would be apportioned out among the cars. We would then caravan to Rainbow Lake.

Once there, our mothers would stay with us at the pool while the men and our grandparents headed for the picnic grounds to unload the cars, set up the tables and start the fire for the steaks.

We loved the pool, which sloped very gently from less than a foot of water to a depth of four feet at the ropes that separated the shallow and deep ends. The pool deck was surrounded by sand, which provided a soft surface on which to place our beach towels, and the little ones played in it with their buckets and shovels. Before the advent of the sissified vinyl float toys or the hoked-up "sports tubes" of today, we had plain old inner tubes salvaged from discarded tires. They were big enough for us to sit inside them, arms trailing out over the water and legs dangling over their sides. The inner tubes of bus or truck tires were especially prized, because these would accommodate several of us.

Eventually, the smell of charcoal-broiling meat would overpower the smell of the chlorine in the water. Daddy or one of the uncles would signal from the picnic grounds that dinner was ready, and we'd change into dry clothes in the dressing rooms and go down to eat. After dinner, the grown-ups would sit around and drink while the kids went to the pavilion to play the juke box and dance. Adrienne still remembers the words to the song that we kept playing one afternoon:

"Shoo-fly pie and apple pandowdy
Makes your eyes light up and your tummy say 'howdy'!
Shoo-fly pie and apple pandowdy
I'll never get enough of that wonderful stuff!"

THEY STAYED AWHILE

Nana and Paw-Paw were no slouches when it came to honoring the Southern tradition of welcoming family members for lengthy visits.

JOHN

In 1940, Uncle Jack and Aunt Cassie shipped their four-year-old John to Poplar Street shortly before their son Jim was born, thus preventing John from irreparably marring what would otherwise remain a blessed event.

John was the undisputed apple of Nana's eye. When her adult children gathered around the dinner table, it was with the certain knowledge that Nana would instantly shush any conversation they might be enjoying should John desire to make a pronouncement. Jo Ann, John's wife, contends that this ruined him for life.

Uncle Dut and Aunt Leeze were engaged at the time of John's visit, and Nana would insist that he accompany them on their dates as a chaperone. They'd go to a movie, sitting with John between them, then head for their favorite bar with their moral deterrent in tow. They'd perch him atop a barstool and order him a coke, overriding John's command to "Make mine Bud!" They'd then slip into a booth to get some private time together while John traded witticisms with the barflies.

John's childhood barhopping continued after his return to Washington. He and his father would hit the neighborhood pub after attending eleven o'clock Mass on Sunday mornings, seldom returning home before two in the afternoon. Aunt Cassie was of another faith, and thought nothing of their lengthy absence since her own church services lasted for several hours. John said it took her five years to figure out what was going on, and that was only because she converted to Catholicism and realized that the Sunday liturgy rarely lasted longer than an hour.

John was the ring-bearer in Uncle Dut's and Aunt Leeze's wedding, meandering down the aisle and chatting up the guests he recognized. He appeared to regard the ring, luckily sewn tightly to its pillow, as an afterthought.

It had almost become necessary to call in an understudy. John had been quite sick throughout the previous night with an upset stomach and it was questionable as to whether he'd recover by showtime. During the party held at Poplar Street the night before, John had helped himself to most of the peanuts that had been set out. However, beets had been served at dinner, and it was these that John blamed for his tribulations. To this day he still gorges on peanuts, but he never touched another beet.

MARILOU AND SHERRY

One of our fondest memories is of the time when Marilou and Sherry stayed with us while Aunt Leeze and Uncle Dut were away on an extended trip. While their brother Justin was left in the care of Bobba, Aunt Leeze's mother, Marilou and Sherry camped out with us on the third floor. A festive atmosphere prevailed.

Sherry, who was by far the most responsible of the four of us, had an unfortunate habit of heeding Daddy's first wake-up call.

"Y'all!" Sherry would hiss. "Wake up!"

Nothing.

"Y'all! If you don't get up, Papa Kev's gonna be MAD!"

"Oh, for God's sake, Sherry! Go back to sleep!"

It took us almost a week to convince her that it wasn't until his third bellow, when he started up the stairs, that anybody had to seriously consider getting out of bed. We were relieved when Sherry finally caught on, as it added a much-needed fifteen minutes to our collective beauty rest.

We never got Sherry to buy into the ironclad rule that beds were not to be made. While we looked on with a mixture of disbelief and exasperation, she'd fuss over the sheets and blankets, making sure that everything was properly tucked in with perfect hospital corners. And to this day, Adrienne and Michele don't make their beds unless company's coming.

MADGE

Another long-term house guest was Madge Reedy, Aunt Ding's sister, who stayed with us for some months after leaving the Dominican order of nuns that she'd joined straight out of high school. One night in 1955, she left her convent in Nashville and didn't return—or, in the language of the time, she "leapt over the wall". Our memories are blurred on what happened next. Adrienne thinks that she called Daddy from a phone booth, asking him if he'd come and get her. Michele thinks that the initial call came from Madge's Mother Superior, telling Daddy that Madge had disappeared. Maybe both memories are accurate. Whatever the case, the next thing we knew was that Daddy was on his way to Nashville to retrieve her.

At the time, a nun had to remain in a cloistered environment while waiting for the Vatican to officially release her from her vows, and Madge was already in the hole on that one. Somehow, the rules were bent. We were not privy to what fabrications Daddy invented to convince which ecclesiastical authorities that 1234 Poplar qualified as a cloistered environment. Suffice it to say that they must have fallen on credulous ears, since Madge was allowed to stay with us until Rome spoke.

All of us sought out Madge's company, as she was a wonderful storyteller with a good sense of humor. Kevitt laughingly claims that Madge ruined his life by bothering to teach him arithmetic and reading in advance of first grade. The two of them would sit on the living room sofa during these sessions and Madge, who'd taught young children for years, very much enjoyed having a pupil as bright and attentive as Kevitt was. However, when he actually started school, he found that he already knew everything that Sister Ruth Agnes was trying to teach. So, as Kevitt puts it, "they mistook me for Stephen Hawking and made me skip a grade". He was put into second grade while still only five years old.

THE ALL-NIGHT MARATHONS

Poplar Street's third floor was an ideal venue for the overnight gatherings of friends that were then called "slumber parties". This was a misnomer, since the last thing any of the participants had in mind was sleeping. We'd sit around in our pajamas and eat, gossip, talk about boys, play records on the old 45rpm turntable, teach each other the latest dances, and eat some more. The reigning food fad at the time, now a classic, was the dip concocted from dried onion soup mix and sour cream. We consumed it by the gallon with bags upon bags of potato chips. Running in tandem with the dip's popularity was pizza, a relatively new but warmly welcomed arrival on the Memphis culinary scene.

When Adrienne was in college and especially in medical school, she frequently got together with class-mates for study sessions. These started when she took physics one summer at what is now the University of Memphis. Instead of having a week to work out a problem with all the illustrations and calculations which the professor required, the students had only one day. This meant they had to collaborate if the assignment was to be completed on time. The class would adjourn to Poplar Street, break the problem down into segments, divvy them up with each person working out a particular aspect of it, then share the wealth.

The dining room table was the venue of choice for the medical students with whom Adrienne would study. There would be nights before important exams when they'd gather to quiz each other and research answers until they fell into exhausted sleep.

One morning, Michele came downstairs and fol-lowed a rumbling noise into the living room, which resembled the depot scene from *Gone With the Wind*. Bodies of sleeping males were strewn from one end of the room to the other, their snores resonating throughout the house.

Since Michele had just left Adrienne sleeping upstairs, another potential chapter in Poplar Street's history of notoriety met a quiet death. Nevertheless, we can technically say that we both spent the night with her medical school class.

VISITORS UNSEEN

Residing on a busy street with no children in our immediate vicinity and our elderly neighbors some distance away, we didn't experience Halloween as our peers did. We did, however, experience at random times throughout the year Halloween's ages-old tradition of the dead walking among the living: we were convinced that Poplar Street was haunted.

We came to this conclusion as being the only possible explanation for the mysterious noises with which our spectral visitors manifested themselves. Besides, Chris swore there was a cold spot on the second floor stair landing.

Though our ghosts were friendly, it became obvious over time that they were they were impossible to train and they never performed on cue—leaving the house with no future as a venue for either séances or parapsychology investigations.

There were three separate answers that Daddy and Mother had at the ready whenever thuds and creaks became ominous.

Answer Number One: "Old houses creak ALL the time."

Answer Number Two: "You're just hearing street noises."

Answer Number Three: "Would you please quit talking like that? You're going to lower the real estate value of the house!" Answer Number Three came up more often when Daddy began to think that maybe there *was* something going on.

To be sure, there were plenty of explainable noises in the house. Frequently, they were produced by the air conditioners. Window air-conditioners were not in widespread use at that time, and understandably so. They were bulky, ugly, and noisy. Eventually, we had them all over Poplar Street, and the one in our bedroom was especially crotchety. It had the ability to produce ten different sounds that mimicked someone breaking into the house.

Adrienne had a system for dealing with this. When the air-conditioner's discordant "THWANNG!" was loud enough, it would awaken her. Adrienne, frightened but not yet frightened enough to wake up everybody else and possibly look like a fool, would urgently whisper, "Michele!"

"PSSST! MICHELE!" She'd keep it up until Michele, a sound sleeper, would stir.

"MICHELE!"

"Mmmph—wassamatter—-huh?"

"Did you hear that noise?"

"What noise?" Michele would now be fully awake. They'd both lie there for a few minutes, listening intently. When the noise failed to recur, Adrienne would go back to sleep, safe in the assurance that the National Guard Was Alert. Michele might lie awake for an hour, alternately listening for the burglar and thinking up ways to kill Adrienne that would appear accidental.

One fall morning before dawn, the windows were open and Adrienne heard the sound of footsteps rustling through the leaves in the yard below. She crept to the window, saw a flashlight beam moving across the ground, and screamed. A plaintive voice called up,

"Adrienne, quit hollering! It's just me, Billy, the paper boy!"

The summer after Paw-Paw died, the air-conditioner in our bedroom was on the fritz. On one particularly hot night, when both Nana and Adrienne were away, Michele relocated to Nana's bedroom. It adjoined Chris's and Kevitt's, and the door between the two rooms was slightly ajar. Michele, Kevitt and Chris were exchanging views about death and ghosts and things that go bump—or not—in the night. Her brothers took pains to remind her that she was sleeping in the same bed in which Paw-Paw had died: Michele was unconcerned, figuring that Paw-Paw wouldn't have harmed her when he was alive, and certainly wouldn't in death. After they settled down to sleep, they heard the unmistakable, strange suction noise that Paw-Paw tended to make in his last days.

"Y'all cut it out!" Michele exclaimed irritably. "I'm trying to go to sleep."

A silence followed, then Chris said: "That wasn't us."

This statement was followed by a LONG silence, then suddenly everybody was up flipping on the lights. Michele went to wake up Mother. Mother dismissed it as a "noise from the street" after she was told what happened.

Michele, suddenly uneasy, asked Mother if she'd sleep in the other bed just for the night.

"Heavens, no!" said Mother, laughing nervously. "I have four children to raise!" It didn't seem the time to remind her that she needn't worry, since three of them were about to die of fright and the fourth was way beyond her control anyway.

Michele retreated to the third floor's stuffy quarters, though she can't remember why she thought that would be any safer.

On another memorable occasion, Adrienne was awakened by the crash of breaking glass. Immediately realizing that this was neither the air-conditioner toying with her nor "a noise from the street", she jumped out of bed and ran to the top of the stairs, yelling for Daddy. To her surprise, he was already starting downstairs, baseball bat in hand; he'd heard it, too. He found no broken windows or broken glass, and called the police. They inspected the entire property and found no evidence of anything amiss, but we all knew we'd heard that glass break.

There were other possible causes for the weird noises. One theory held that metal hair rollers and even the fillings in one's teeth could, under the right conditions, pick up noises from radio transmissions. But we didn't want science encroaching on a good story, and dismissed the idea that we might have been wired for sound.

We like to think that even the disembodied were entertained within Poplar Street's walls, as our visitors all had their own ways of enriching our lives. In the company of all those characters, the good times rolled, the laughter came easily, and the stories unfolded over the years. We wish now that we'd paid more attention: We had no idea that the memories we were creating might one day enable us to give expression to voices now silenced.

PART THREE

POPLAR STREET IN ORDINARY TIME

Potpourri of Hours

Sunday mornings, childhood amusements

and one sadistic dentist

Celebrations

Santa's boot, golden eggs

and fallen angels

The Music of Poplar Street

Strange coincidences, and why

the Poplar Street house was banned

POTPOURRI OF HOURS

In between the earthquakes, the visitors and both real and imagined ghosts, Poplar Street served up a variety of experiences which linger like confetti in the memories of growing up. We would deal with doll collections, childhood games, Sunday mornings, and play with a host of much-loved cousins. That was Poplar Street in ordinary time—except that it never felt ordinary.

SUNDAY MORNINGS ON POPLAR STREET

Every Sunday it was a given that we'd attend Sunday Mass. However, the logistics of doing so varied constantly throughout our years at Poplar Street. After Nana parted company with St. Peter's choir in 1948, she and Paw-Paw would always attend the 8:00 Mass at Sacred Heart. Daddy would accompany them, as would whichever of us were still too young to protest. Aunt Dokey's family lived within walking distance of the church in the Court Street apartments, and also attended this Mass until they moved to their home on York Street and into another parish.

We always sat in "our" pew, the one donated by our great-grandfather. It bore a small brass plaque with a number on it, which we can no longer remember, and this was how we recognized it.

Paw-Paw helped with taking up the collection; Daddy assisted with this also when there was a no-show among the regulars. Daddy enjoyed shaking the collection basket pointedly under the faces of those who weren't contributing. Embarrassed, they'd grudgingly reach into their pockets and hand over the goods. Daddy preened over his success in parting these "deadbeats" from their money.

Much as we might have liked to duck out of church early, we always stayed until the bitter end because of Paw-Paw's scrupulosity and Nana's love of belting out the closing hymn. Her soaring voice dominated all the punier ones in the congregation as she pealed her way through *Holy God, We Praise Thy Name*. While she reveled in the attention when half the church turned to stare at her, we wanted to crawl under the pew.

After Mass, Daddy would drive our grandparents home and then take us to Winkler's Bakery, one of our favorite places. There, Daddy would get the fan-tan rolls for Sunday dinner while we'd pick out all sorts of pastries, cakes and gooey stuff, which we'd spend the next few days eating. We were primed from childhood to be cholesterites, a transcendent state of being though not an actual word.

Bill Rowe used to marvel at the "treats" available at
Poplar Street. In addition to Winkler's delicacies, gone
within days, ice cream was always on hand. Bill and
his sister Carol frequently accompanied Aunt Dokey
when she came to visit Nana. Lest they eavesdrop on
their elders' private chat, they'd be banished to the
kitchen with orders to get themselves some ice cream.
On one of these visits, shortly after Nana's and Paw-
Paw's golden anniversary celebration, they opened
the freezer to discover a bonanza. Left over from the
party were a number of packages, each containing ten
4x4 bricks of vanilla ice cream surrounding what were
probably orange sherbet "bells". Bill says that he and
Carol each devoured about six or seven servings. To his
knowledge, no one was ever the wiser.

Upon our return from Winkler's a large Sunday
breakfast would await us, with the dining room table
set formally and a glass of orange juice at every place.
Nana required the maid to work a half-day on Sundays,
to prepare both this breakfast and the Sunday dinner
which would be held in the early afternoon, frequently
with the extended family in attendance.

During breakfast, Nana would conduct a critique
of the church service we'd all attended, focusing on the
sermon and the appearances of her fellow parishioners.
There were always those who "looked like hell". There
was always some poor woman whom Nana deemed
"tacky", pointing out the lack of taste evident in the
woman's choice of dress and hat. Paw-Paw would then
remember something about the family of the tacky

person, and the conversation would turn on that for awhile. Occasionally, Paw-Paw would feel called upon to defend the tacky person's honor, at which point Nana would interrupt him with, "Oh, just be still!"

Mother wouldn't participate in any of it. She'd go to the 10:30 Mass alone, though Adrienne or Michele might go with her on the infrequent occasions when it suited them. We later found out that there was speculation in the parish about whether Daddy was a widower because he was never there with a wife.

This speculation was not confined to Sacred Heart Church. One of Michele's dates had also commented that he thought Daddy was a widower, since Mother had never come downstairs to meet him. Mother so rarely met any of our boyfriends that the only ones she actually knew were either those we'd been seeing for awhile or those whom Daddy was convinced were going to turn us into Fallen Women.

Mother trusted Daddy's judgment in this regard. Daddy relished the confrontational aspect of meeting our dates, which harkened back to the days when Aunt Ding was so popular with the boys. Daddy generally grilled any potential boyfriend who came to call on her, and made the point to one unfortunate young man that he needed to "be careful with the driving—we've had a number of wrecks here lately."

The guy flippantly responded, "Well, we all have to die some time!"

Daddy wheeled around and hissed, "Do you think I care whether YOU die or not? I'm talking about HER!"

Aunt Ding was red-faced, but Daddy had discovered a new skill, which he further honed in later years on behalf of his daughters.

But we digress.

As we grew older, we were usually out too late on Saturday nights to drag ourselves to the 8 a.m. Mass. But it was the institution of the Sunday noon Masses throughout the diocese which ensured that we'd never darken the church doors any earlier if there was a way to avoid it. Even so, Adrienne still needed a challenge to motivate her, so she started "seeing how close I can cut it." If we had to leave at 11:50, she'd start getting dressed at 11:40.

Sometimes we would venture downstairs for the family breakfast, usually looking like what Daddy called "the morning after the night before". Daddy would give us the once-over, roll his eyes heavenward and piously intone, "If the Lord forgives me, I'll never take another drink!"

One year, in anticipation of Father's Day, Daddy wondered whether we'd be attending the 8 a.m. Mass. We all declined in a flurry of creative excuses. Somewhat bitterly, he said, "Well, I know one time we'll all be in church together. My funeral!"

His comment penetrated our self-absorbed fog, shaming us into a command performance. On that Father's Day we were there, "dressed fit to kill" so somebody else's Nana couldn't say we looked awful, and wishing there was a sunglasses concession outside the church. Daddy seemed so proud and happy, and after Mass was boasting to everyone, "See? I have all four of them here today!" —-as if nobody could count.

Not long after breakfast, the mouth-watering aroma of beef roasting in the oven would begin wafting throughout the house, signaling the impending arrival of aunts, uncles and cousins.

Surrounded as we were by institutions, we had no experience of a normal neighborhood ambience and had no neighborhood playmates. When Nana and Paw-Paw first moved the family to Poplar Street, Aunt Ding remembers being very lonely, as she had no one her own age to keep her company. She had no friends until she started school. We never felt this deprivation, as we had our cousins, whose ages and interests mirrored our own.

CHILDHOOD AMUSEMENTS ON POPLAR STREET

While the adults engaged in their boring grown-up conversations, we occupied ourselves with all sorts of games and activities. There being no shortage of imagination among our ranks, some of these we'd dream up on the spot. We'd have "talent contests", which consisted of taking turns singing favorite songs, and which Michele and Sherry frequently won since they were the best singers. Their record of wins might have gone unbroken, except that consideration was also given to interpretation, costuming and what's now called "presentation", at which the older girls held a slight edge. The costumes for these shows were fairly inventive, considering that they were fashioned from either whatever we happened to be wearing, rear-ranged more artfully with the help of a few safety pins, or from whatever we could scavenge: towels, sheets, fabric remnants, and the tinfoil we used to make tiaras.

On warm days, the outdoors beckoned with the prospect of making mud pies, climbing the mag-nolia tree or playing house beneath its low-hanging branches. We made castles and tunnels in the sandbox and pedaled the swings to ever-greater heights. There were many games of hide-and-seek, tag, Mother-May-I and hopscotch. The broad sidewalk that fronted Poplar was ideal for roller-skating or riding our bikes.

We climbed as high as we could inside the sawdust vent at William R. Moore School next door, then slid down into the deep pile of sawdust curls. It was only by lucky chance that no one ever activated the vent while we were climbing around inside it.

After the murder of a young woman in the early 1950s directly across from the house, our outdoor ventures included being on the lookout for the perp, something we'd smugly decided we were qualified to do. Whenever we played in front of the house, we'd go into vigilante mode; this meant taking note of anybody who looked suspicious, which in our minds appeared to be everybody. The case was never solved, but we were fascinated that news accounts on the early television stations featured the Poplar Street house in the background.

Inspired by the annual May Processions at Sacred Heart Church, we'd have our own May Processions in honor of the Virgin Mary, which could get elaborate. We'd decorate some old side table as an altar, overlaying it with a white dish towel. We'd adorn it with streamers of lace and ribbon which we begged off Mother and Nana, who were at a loss to refuse our sanctimoniously-delivered requests for "something to make Mary's altar pretty". We set out juice glasses of sweetheart roses picked off the bush in the front yard, and in the midst of these we'd place our statue of Mary. We'd draw straws to see who got to place the tinfoil crown on her head, and tie a bedsheet around the chosen one to simulate a royal robe signifying her status. We'd make ourselves bouquets of dandelions, clover blossoms and more roses, and then march around the yard singing May hymns for a suitable amount of time before the actual crowning.

Michele says that we once had a contest to see who could design the best wedding finery. Adrienne, who has no memory of it, was the judge. It seems that Adrienne decided that Michele had created the best underwear, which caused Michele to pitch a fit because she'd actually entered the design in the wedding veil category.

Charades was a favorite game. Mimi had a gift for coming up with profound and generally obscure sayings for her competitors to act out. One of these, "The sting of a reproach is the truth of it", stuck with Michele for years.

Mimi's tonsillectomy when she was five occasioned many games of "Operation". The surgical theater was recreated on the front porch, with an old canvas deck chair, turned upside down, serving as the operating table. Mimi's memories of her experience were sharp and detailed. Thanks to her coaching, Marilou and Adrienne could perform capably as either the patient, the anesthesiologist, the nurse or the surgeon. At the end of the "operation", the surgeon and the anesthesiologist would become the orderlies. They'd move the patient from the deck chair to the concrete porch ledge, where she'd recuperate. In looking back, we were fortunate that leeches weren't still in use.

We spent a lot of time playing with the Kershugs, so named because one of the books that we enjoyed having Paw-Paw read to us involved a frog who popped up out of a well. The frog's emergence from the well was captioned, "And a voice said, KERSHUG!" We were beguiled with both the word and the way Paw-Paw boomed it out, so it was a foregone conclusion that we'd find some way to incorporate it into everyday usage.

An eminently forgettable board game called *Elopement* proved to be the vehicle. Though we had no interest in how it was played, the pieces that went with it immediately captured our imaginations. There were four sets of two-inch high plastic figures, each set including a bride, a groom, a mother and a father. There was a red set, a blue set, a green one and a yellow one. We named them The Kershugs, and they were prized instruments for enacting a variety of scenarios, most of which involved the antics of royalty. Our delusions of grandeur knew no bounds.

Another favorite game was Dropping Notes, which involved pretending that we were in situations that required us to send messages. Foreshadowing the advent of text-messagingl, half of us would sit on the floor in the upstairs hall at the top of the open staircase and drop urgent notes, attached to thread, over the railing to the other half sitting below. This had an advantage in that it required only two people to get a dialogue going.

Televisions sets were starting to become a staple in American households in 1950. Among our favorite programs was Buck Rogers, who was the captain of a spaceship that explored the galaxy. We adopted Buck, who took us on a number of imaginary trips into outer space. Our spaceship, constructed on the side porch, was made of the wicker chairs which we overturned, arranged in a circle and covered with chenille bedspreads. The chairs were so large that we each had our own room, and the circle arrangement created a common area. We went to Jupiter, Mars, and Saturn and Venus; the moon was deemed too close to be of much interest, and we needed the whole afternoon to get to Uranus or Pluto. Somehow, Adrienne always got to be Buck's girlfriend, Wilma. Nobody ever saw Buck, because Adrienne relayed his messages.

Like most of our peers, we liked to play with dolls. Unlike most of them, we were bored with baby dolls because the opportunities for featuring them in the adventurous fantasies that we loved were severely limited. When Adrienne was about four, she wanted a "bride doll" for Christmas. Mother's interpretation of this consisted of procuring an almost life-sized baby doll and inexplicably dressing it as a bride. Adrienne was disgusted.

Though it was hard to make the flat-figured dolls of that era look like grown-ups, we did our best. Nana would give us her unwanted scarves and costume jewelry, and these were our tools. Adrienne figured out a way to make evening gowns out of these scarves by draping the silk and securing it with a clip-on earring, a technique that later turned out to have useful applications. When she was a penniless college freshman in New Orleans and needed a costume for a Halloween party, Adrienne dyed a sheet black, draped it on herself the same way she'd draped the scarves on our dolls, and called herself—appropriately enough—a vampire. Judging from the current gothic craze (circa 2010), we now know that Adrienne was born several generations too soon.

Among the dolls that we owned were around fifteen "storybook" dolls by Madame Alexander. For the longest time, we weren't allowed to play with these, which we found frustrating. Uncle Jake, Mother's brother-in-law who was a skilled carpenter, even built us a cabinet with glass doors in which to house them.

We found out the hard way that once any of our dolls' clothes or hair were rearranged, it wasn't possible to restore the hair or clothing to its original bandbox appearance. This was particularly true of the storybook dolls, which were only eight inches high and particularly vulnerable to mussing. One day when Mother was out shopping, we succumbed to the temptation to play with some of them. Thinking that there was no turning back, Mother gave up and let us have at it. The end result was that a collection of dolls that would have been worth thousands today was gradually ruined.

Another victim of ignorance was Chris's collection of baseball cards, which would have been worth many times more than the storybook dolls had they survived. Over a period of years, Chris had avidly accumulated so many of these that they'd have overflowed a standard 22" carry-on bag. We think that they were literally swept up in some over-zealous housecleaning effort.

Kevitt's stamp collection, however, has somehow endured to this day. It escaped the casualty list possibly because Kevitt moved out with it before it was washed away in the waves of yard sales that followed Nana's death. At one point, he was quite intent upon his hobby. He'd rummage through Paw-Paw's desk, looking for old letters with affixed stamps that he could pilfer. This was a source of consternation to Paw-Paw, whose desk was his personal Holy of Holies to which no one, not even Nana, was allowed entry. Kevitt also came close to re-igniting an old family donnybrook

when his stamp search took him to a box in the basement containing telegrams documenting the specifics
of the unpleasantness.

In his enthusiasm, Kevitt would send off for
stamps to companies that advertised in Boys' Life
magazine, but his handwriting was such that his letter
"K" looked more like an "R", and the stamps would
arrive addressed to "Revitt Adler". We wondered if
the stamp company thought that Kevitt might be a
frog with a name that sounded like a croak, a possibility we found hilarious. Then, we were so entertained
by the Dear Revitt letters from the stamp company
begging him for reimbursement that we didn't realize
they were dunning letters. In retrospect, we assume
that Kevitt's credit rating was not later affected by
Revitt's financial indiscretions.

With the current market value of 1950s Madame
Alexander dolls, now-rare baseball cards and authen-
tic Victorian wicker, perhaps our great-grandfather's
sale of downtown Memphis real estate for a pittance
marked the beginning of a trend. In a world where
people are accused of knowing the cost of everything
and the value of nothing, we can confirm that Poplar
Street didn't know either.

Except for Kevitt.

DOCTORS AND DENTISTS

Where medical assistance was concerned, Poplar
Street was a mixed bag.

Our pediatricians were outstanding. Dr. Tom Mitchell, who later went on to head the Department of Pediatrics at the University of Tennessee Medical School, visited the sickbeds of our childhoods back in the gone forever days when doctors made house calls. As soon as Mother gravely announced that Dr. Tom was coming, Adrienne and Michele—no matter how sick—would plot strategy: "You kick him, and I'll bite!" At one point, Michele thought she would be safe if she just hid beneath the covers, but Dr. Mitchell was used to camouflage.

All of the cousins went to Dr. Mitchell or to one of his partners, Dr. James Etteldorf and Dr. George Love-joy. Some went for as long as they could get away with it. When Marilou discovered that a physical exam was required for entrance into college, she adamantly refused to see anyone but Dr. Mitchell. At the time, pediatricians didn't usually see patients over the age of sixteen, but no amount of coaxing could induce Marilou to change her mind. Aunt Leeze gave up and called his office.

"And how old is your daughter, Mrs. Adler?" asked the receptionist.

Aunt Leeze took a deep breath and replied, "Eighteen."

There was a pause at the other end of the line. "Um, I'm afraid she's a little OLD for us to be seeing her…"

Aunt Leeze, long past the point of embarrassment, begged shamelessly.

Dr. Mitchell saw Marilou.

These doctors were the exceptions. Some of the other practitioners our family consulted brought to mind the days when tobacco smoke enemas were considered the treatment of choice for the attempted resuscitation of drowning victims.

One specialist we consulted was actually fairly competent, and we were disappointed when he was "brought up on a morals charge", as the euphemism had it. Apparently, there was no way he could explain some pictures of himself that surfaced, and he suffered a permanently tarnished reputation as a result. Nowadays, of course, he'd have his own reality show.

We don't remember who was responsible for bringing Dr.X on board our own little Good Ship Hope.

When Adrienne was in her sixth quarter of medical school, she came home one afternoon to learn from Nana that Daddy had become ill and that Dr. X had just arrived to see him. Adrienne ran upstairs and went into Daddy's room in time to hear Dr. X commenting that there was "a lot of flu going around". He then asked Daddy when he started to feel sick.

"Well, I was driving down East Parkway, taking my son to school, and all of a sudden I felt my left arm and left leg go weak…"

"Yep, that's the flu, all right!" Dr. X opined.

Apparently unconcerned, he scribbled out a prescription for an antibiotic, handed it to Mother, and left. Adrienne was appalled; when she checked Daddy's blood pressure, she found that it was dangerously elevated at 240/140. Adrienne immediately called one of her professors, a cardiologist, who admitted Daddy to the hospital with a stroke. With that episode, medical care and the odds for survival around Poplar Street started to improve.

Improve, that is, if we exclude the family dentists.

Mother was determined to find a dentist who would be gentle with her offspring and sensitive to their fears. In her zeal to locate such a gem, she managed to come up with a Jekyll-Hyde type who, from our perspective, may as well have graduated from dental school at Auschwitz under Mengele.

Dr. Y surreptitiously loathed children in general and us in particular. We were certain that Dr. Y became a dentist in order to legally torture little kids, even though it meant stopping short of killing and eating them since this would involve risking the electric chair. When Adrienne was five, she had a cavity in one of her molars that Dr. Y filled without benefit of Novocain. Adrienne said it felt as though Dr. Y was trying to drill a hole through the bottom of her foot, but being the paragon of virtue that she was, sat there and took it.

Michele labored under no such constraints. The first time Dr. Y came at her with a malevolent look and a sharp instrument, Michele fought back with her own favorite weapon which, ironically, was her mouthful of teeth. As Michele watched smugly, Dr. Y stalked into the waiting room where Mother was sitting and icily informed her that "I will not treat That Child again."

Michele's triumph was short-lived, thanks to Mother's misguided entreaties that her daughter be allowed to continue as a patient. Dr. Y later filled eleven cavities in Michele's mouth over a three-month period, all of them cold turkey. Along about the 9th cavity, Michele was crying for Novocain. Dr. Y said that Mother would have to "authorize" it. Mother, who had never had a cavity filled and couldn't understand what the problem was, said OK. A crestfallen Dr. Y made a pretense of accepting Mother's permission, then proceeded to give Michele what must have been a placebo while continuing to ignore her cries of agony. To this day, Michele remembers the odd smile on Dr. Y's face that accompanied the words, "You've been given an anesthetic. Not my fault if it isn't working."

By then, Michele had become something of a malpractice magnet. When she was born, the nurses at the hospital thought she was adorable and kept putting little ribbons in her hair to show her off in the nursery. Apparently, they were having so much fun with her that they forgot to feed her, and her near-death from dehydration effectively ended her career as show dog for the hospital's newborn division. The long amateur night of Michele's infancy did not end when she was

taken home to Poplar Street. The nurse hired to help
care for her had her own off-the-books treatment for
prickly heat, which consisted of popping the blisters
with a needle. Luckily for Michele, Daddy happened
to walk in during one of the "treatment" sessions and
fired the nurse on the spot.

That notwithstanding, Michele was in her 40s
before she could walk into a dentist's office without starting to cry. Adrienne was in her fifties
before she could go the two days prior to a dental
appointment without having immediate access to a
bathroom.

There was another dentist used by some in the
family for reasons that remain unclear. With the sham
joviality of a department store Santa, he was a ham-
handed sort with a creative technique for adminis-
tering Novocain that might render one's entire nose
numb, while leaving the tooth he was drilling totally
unaffected.

We all envied Nana, who had perfect teeth that had
rarely sustained a cavity. On the few occasions when
she developed one, she never required an anesthetic,
and never complained of any pain. Our descendants
should be so lucky as to inherit the Reedy teeth. Many
of us inherited the Adler teeth which, in Paw-Paw's
time, had to be put into a glass at night. Nowadays,
we just walk around with mouths full of crowns
and root canals, and with the quiet satisfaction of
knowing we've put our dentists' children through
college.

Throughout our years on Poplar Street, home remedies were popular. Mother swore by something called Oschner's Solution, an antiseptic so obscure that when she had need of it while on vacation in Miami, the pharmacist we consulted had never heard of it and had to look it up.

Nana believed firmly in alcohol rubs to reduce fever, mustard plasters for something or other, and migrations to better climates if that's what it took. Occasionally someone would bring home a bottle of holy water, which Mother thought would work if sprinkled liberally in the sick room. One time we managed to get a vial of water from Lourdes, which Mother deemed the sine qua non of do-it-yourself cures. She somehow got the idea that it would help with warts, and used it to douse these growths on Michele's knee and later on Kevitt's thumb. The water had no discernible effect— Michele's wart had to be surgically removed— but it's possible that Our Lady of Lourdes had bigger fish to fry.

In retrospect, it was mystifying that we found some of the "Health Care Providers" that we did. Memphis is home to the University of Tennessee Medical Units, at which a number of highly competent, nationally-recognized physicians and dentists teach and practice. Celebrities come from all over the world to Memphis to see specialists who are at the pinnacles of their fields.

But Poplar Street was a primitive little oasis that might have fared better with a shaman, candles, rattles, chants, incantations and your garden variety eye of newt. In fact, we suspect that these may have played a bigger part in the maintenance of our health and welfare than anybody ever dared to mention.

CELEBRATIONS

CHRISTMAS

The mists of time have endowed the Christmases at Poplar Street with a magic that they may or may not have actually possessed. Whatever the case, we still get teary-eyed at the sound of the Robert Shaw Chorale singing a cappella carols. Daddy had the entire collection of their recorded Christmas music, and we played those records non-stop through the holidays.

The season was heralded by the pungent, spicy aromas that filled the house on Fruitcake Day, generally observed sometime over Thanksgiving weekend. Nana would mix up the fruitcake batter in the largest roasting pan available, and would produce about a dozen cakes. Upon their extraction from the oven, she would drench them in large quantities of bourbon, then wrap them first in cheesecloth and then in cellophane so they could "age". They were deemed fully ripened on Christmas Eve, when Daddy dutifully delivered them to the designated recipients.

They were awful.

We agreed in later years that it must have been Nana's fruitcake that gave rise to the rumor that there was only one in existence anywhere, which just kept getting passed around through the years because nobody would eat it. We certainly wouldn't. The only thing that ever surpassed its sheer nastiness was the plum pudding that Daddy had ordered from someplace that should probably remain nameless. Despite everybody else's misgivings, he insisted that "I want to have plum pudding on Christmas Day just once before I die." Michele thought that he may have sensed his impending demise. Adrienne thought he may have been planning it, as the pudding was that bad.

Christmas desserts would have been a complete bust were it not for Mamie's pumpkin pies. Mamie was an outstanding cook: Her pies were ambrosial and her pumpkin pie remains the best we've ever had. It totally outstripped the competition— mostly contributed by Aunt Lizzie, who missed out on the baking gene.

Aunt Lizzie's coconut cake was inedible, its tough layers of flavorless yellow cake held together and topped with a substance reminiscent of bathtub grout. Her chocolate cake was saved from abject failure only by the pecan halves that festooned it. These we picked off and ate when nobody was looking, after carefully ridding them of any icing that adhered. While we could avoid eating what she delivered, we were put on the spot when we visited her. In such circumstances, we were saved by what the family called the Aunt Lizzie Slice, which was one cut so thinly as to be almost transparent. All we had to do was spread whatever it was around the plate so that no one could tell how much had actually made it into our mouths.

The other redeeming dessert consisted of the Frango mints that cousin Mary Jane Reedy sent to us from Marshall Fields in Chicago. These we inhaled. To this day, Frangos mean Christmas—only now, with Marshall Fields lost to the ages, we have to get them from Macy's.

In the annals of the holiday celebrations that took place before our time, one dessert that was removed from the menu at Nana's insistence was a lemon confection that was part cake and part custard. It was baked in individual glass ramekins, and these were turned upside down to cool prior to their unmolding. One Christmas, Nana had whipped some cream with which to top them, but she'd gotten herself tipsy and plopped the whipped cream directly onto the glass ramekins. A family member came into the kitchen as this was happening. She doubled over with laughter, and promptly went out to the living room to broadcast Nana's slip-up to the rest of the assembly. Nana was deeply embarrassed—to the point where it was very rare that we ever saw her having more than one drink, almost always a Dubonnet.

We eagerly anticipated picking out the Christmas tree in mid-December. Daddy would load all of us into the car, and we might visit several lots before finding the perfect tree. Daddy insisted that it reach the ceiling, whose considerable height he unfailingly overestimated. One year, he miscalculated by a good four feet. Instead of paring the tree from the bottom, he decided to save time and sawed off the top, leaving a trapezoidal hunk of pine branches that looked more like a mulch pile than a Christmas tree. It took him three hours, cursing and swearing all the while, to shape it into something that the decorations could more or less disguise.

Our trees were usually Scotch pines. One year we got a blue spruce, which must have been harvested in July. There was a steady tick-tick-ticking as its needles gave up the ghost and fell onto the bare hardwood floor. By New Year's Eve, it was completely barren. That was the first and last time that we deviated from the norm.

Because the trees were so tall, they were prone to fall over under the weight of the three hundred standard-sized lights and the numerous ornaments. To minimize this possibility, Daddy fashioned a "stand". He set an iron pipe in a large galvanized washtub, then poured concrete around the pipe to a level of about seven inches. It weighed a ton but did the job, aided by the twine with which we further secured the trees to the nails we drove into the woodwork.

The tub lasted until 1970, when it sprung a leak. By that time, Daddy was getting tired of the whole monumental operation and was ready to junk the newly-purchased tree out-of-hand. Kevitt and Chris saved Christmas and the tree with the suggestion that they go out and buy a bigger tub to house the leaky one, which they did, but that was the last real tree anyone would see at Poplar Street. The next year, Daddy converted to artificial ones.

Decorating the house for Christmas always followed the same pattern. The first things to go up were the tall electric candles in the windows and the red bulbs in the living room wall sconces, around which were fastened transparent bells and ribbons. Next, Daddy would put up the outdoor lights around the front porch, while Mother arranged the Nativity set on the mantel.

Last of all came the tree. It was brought into the house around December 20th, and it took a full evening just to get it into its stand and upright. Everyone had an opinion about whether it leaned to the right or to the left, about which of its aspects should face in what direction, about how many inches it needed to be moved forward, backward or sideways. It generally remained in the position it occupied at the point when Daddy finally got bored listening to all of us. Even in its unadorned state, the tree transformed the house, perfuming it with its lovely, piney, Christmassy scent.

It took another full evening to string the lights. No matter how carefully we'd tried to pack them away the previous year, they somehow managed to get hopelessly tangled in the intervening months. The only possible explanation was that they'd spent the time mating. It took awhile to get them separated, to replace burnt-out bulbs, and to make sure that none of the wires had frayed or otherwise acquired arson potential.

Getting the lights onto the tree was fraught with peril. The procedure consisted of standing on the ladder, holding onto it with one hand while stretching in toward the tree and getting a bulb into position with the other. Accomplishing this task without risking catastrophe required cold sobriety, which is why Adrienne was assigned to do it at an age which would have qualified her for Child Protective Services in the 21st century. That she emerged every year miraculously unscathed was attributable only to the grace of God and dumb animal luck.

After the lights, the ornaments were easy. We had some beautiful ones, most of which didn't survive. This was because when Adrienne moved into her first house, Daddy decided to give her the ones she liked best. This was obviously a unilateral decision on his part, as he had no idea how to pack them for shipping and most were in shards by the time Adrienne received them.

The tree's final touch was the tinsel, always called icicles, which Mother insisted be applied one strand at a time. Clumps were considered tacky, and we could never let it be said that we had a tacky tree. It wasn't enough to just place the strands on the branches. No, we had to TOSS them, so they'd look "spontaneous."

Adrienne and Michele were quite practiced in the technique. There had been a chandelier in our bedroom with extended arms, and we'd had hours of fun with a game we'd invented that involved throwing our underwear up toward the chandelier, aiming for one of the arms. Points were scored for each success. One night, Mother came in and caught us doing it. She ended up joining the fun, though her height advantage disqualified her from competition. The icicle toss had a similar cachet to it.

Sometimes we blanketed the tree with artificial snow, but it required so much snow and made such a mess that we generally dispensed with this nicety. Finally, Mother would surround the base of the tree with old bedsheets and cover them with cotton batting. This arrangement extended up onto the bay window seat behind the tree, leaving plenty of room for all the gifts that arrived both from and for the extended family.

At some point, these gifts became so numerous and demanded so many hours of shopping from all the aunts that an edict came down from on high that we were to draw names. All of the cousins immediately grasped that this would severely curtail our annual haul of loot, but our whining fell on deaf ears.

One year, we decided that we wanted a tree of our very own in the third floor den. We picked out one that had been sprayed silver, and which gave off an odd metallic odor after its lights had been burning for awhile. Since both of us had always found taking down the Christmas decorations to be a singularly dreary endeavor, we decided to postpone the dismantling of the little tree until it wouldn't be so depressing. The tree remained standing until the Wednesday before Easter, when we arrived home from school to find a trail of silver pine needles marking the tree's progress down three flights of steps, through the kitchen and out the back door. Mother was waiting for us. All she said was, "Clean it up." After that, we elected to make do with the big tree downstairs, thus aborting our first attempt at independence.

We don't remember when Santa Claus stopped visiting. We presume it was when Mother and Daddy no longer had the stamina to stay up most of Christmas Eve doing the honors, only to be wrested from sleep at the crack of dawn by our excited gibbering as we raced downstairs to see what Santa had left.

Once, when Adrienne was three, she awakened at two a.m. hearing noises, which she immediately attributed to Santa. As quietly as she could, she crept down the stairs, hoping to get a glimpse of him. Mother and Daddy were sitting on the sofa, drinks in hand, and spotted her. As it happened, they'd just finished laying out the presents.

"Look!" Mother cried, thinking fast. "Santa's going up the chimney!"

They had Adrienne convinced that she'd seen one of Santa's boots as he made his ascent, and Adrienne believed it until the cold light of reason dawned upon her at about age six. However, the story was not wasted, as she milked it for mileage with her own children, who found it fascinating—until the cold light of reason dawned on them, too.

Michele, on the other hand, believed in Santa much longer than most because Adrienne had said that she'd seen Santa's boot going up the chimney. Of course, considering the strange visitors we had at Poplar Street, this did not require a significant stretch of the imagination. The story also kept Kevitt hooked on the Santa myth beyond reasonable expectations. He, of course, passed it along to Chris, who was seven before Daddy could stop spending the wee hours of Christmas Day searching for missing parts of the some-assembly-required toys.

In later years, we opened family gifts after returning from the annual visit with Mother's relatives on Christmas Eve. One year, we decided to have a professional photograph taken of the four of us siblings to give to our parents for Christmas. We set up an appointment to have the picture taken on an evening in early November, and had to sneak our dress clothes out to the car without anyone seeing them. Neither of us sisters could decide what to wear, and our clothes alone filled the back seat, thoroughly annoying Kevitt and Chris. We snapped and growled at one another all the way to the photographer's, but the portrait that resulted from that session somehow captured the best in each of us. When Mother and Daddy opened it, they both wept. It was probably among the best presents that any of us ever gave.

The highlight of Christmas morning was Nana's eggnog, which she'd whip up when the last of the stragglers had returned from Mass. She'd separate a dozen eggs, beat the yolks with a couple of quarts of cream and some sugar, then add at least a pint of bourbon and some nutmeg. She'd make a meringue with the egg whites and stir it in only partially, so that distinct islands of it were visible, and then pour this mixture into water glasses (juice glasses for the little ones) and top each with a very large dollop of whipped cream. After downing one of those concoctions, we'd feel pretty woozy for awhile. The younger children even napped without protest.

Around noontime, our cousins, aunts and uncles would begin arriving. More presents were exchanged and unwrapped. Depending upon our ages at the time, the cousins would fan out into various corners of the house to play, visit, gossip, argue, or conspire until dinner was served around three.

We generally had at least eighteen people gathered in the dining room, either at the main table or at a side table dragged into the room from the kitchen and disguised with holiday linens. The twenty-eight pound turkey would have been in the oven since six that morning, the stuffing baking inside it. All the usual accompaniments were on deck, and all the aunts contributed. Occasionally Mother would make cran-berry sauce, but to this day we prefer the jellied kind that we unmold from the can and cut into slices.

At some point during dinner, Daddy could be counted upon to relate the Depression-era story about how the turkey had been left out on the back porch to keep it cold and somebody stole it. That this had happened at Thanksgiving instead of Christmas was irrelevant, as the tale had a satisfying Bob Cratchit-Tiny Tim ring to it.

Later in the afternoon, we'd hold an impromptu open house, and various friends and relatives would visit. When Marilou and Adrienne were in college at Memphis State, these gatherings underwent considerable expansion. They'd approach Daddy and Uncle Dut and tell them they'd invited "a few friends" to stop by, which was code for "lay in an extra supply of Christmas Cheer." Each year, the number of revelers grew. Before the family finally put on the brakes, things had reached a point where people were walking in off the street, with Adrienne thinking they were Marilou's friends and Marilou thinking they were Adrienne's.

One December, Adrienne decided to renovate the third floor den in time for Christmas. She thought that the college crowd needed its own place to gather, away from the glare of the family spotlight. At the time that she devised the color scheme, she was pulling an all-nighter in preparation for final exams and was in a sleep-deprivation trance. In the light of day—and most especially in the candlelight of night—the rosy red walls and ceiling and the pink corduroy covers on the daybeds positively glowed. Daddy took one look at the finished product and said that it "looked like a Chinese whorehouse". We wondered how he knew.

Another year, a group had returned to Poplar Street for a nightcap after making the rounds of the Christmas parties. Marilou and Adrienne headed for the bar, only to find that the cupboard was bare. Undeterred, they ventured down the rickety basement stairs into the bowels of the house and into Paw-Paw's wine cellar.

Checking the assortment of ancient potables, they found a bottle that appeared promising. They dusted off the cobwebs, brought it up to the kitchen and opened it. The fumes wafting upward smelled suspiciously like vinegar. They looked at each other and shrugged, concluding that given everything else their guests had imbibed that day, they'd never know the difference if the vinegar was disguised with enough ginger ale.

They were right.

When we were young, the remainder of the holidays was spent playing with new toys and visiting with our cousins and friends. As we got older, there were parties every night.

Sometimes, the parties were brought to us. At dawn one morning, we were awakened by caterwauling down in the yard below our bedroom window. Further investigation revealed the presence of three young men of our acquaintance, dressed in somewhat disheveled formal attire and serenading us off-key at the tops of their lungs.

As they brayed on about angels who frequented honky-tonks, the entire household was gradually roused.

By the third verse, Mother stood looking out the window in bewilderment. "Do you think they want money?" she asked plaintively.

THANKSGIVING

This differed from Christmas at Poplar Street in that it occurred a month earlier and was unenlivened by the decorations, the presents, the music, the religious celebrations, the eggnog and the fruitcake. Mincemeat pie, which was eaten by no one except Paw-Paw and the resident dog, pinch-hit for the fruitcake.

Thanksgiving's principal charm was that it marked the official opening of the holiday season. In anticipation of this season, the Catholic girls' high schools of that time and place all suspended classes during the three days leading up to Thanksgiving in favor of holding religious retreats.

Most of us good Catholic girls had only one concern when it came to saving our souls, which was how far we could go with a boy without committing a mortal sin. Our chief aim at these retreats was to pin down the retreat master on this delicate subject without incurring the suspicion that we were "fast", a goal that seemed to remain just out of reach. The nuns knew all of this, of course, and were bound and determined to counter the power of our evil hormones with enough talk of sin and death to safeguard our purity at least until New Year's was over. They must have succeeded to some extent, because we don't recall any emergency Lenten weddings.

EASTER

Being Catholic, we observed all of the Holy Week rituals which led up to big event, Easter Sunday. When we were young, the pageantry that used to be associated with these rituals captivated us, and gave the Feast of the Resurrection a significance that went considerably beyond colored eggs and the magic bunny.

At St. Peter's, selected young children were invited to participate in the processions held on Holy Thursday and Good Friday. And since Nana was the undisputed star of St. Peter's choir, we were among that select few.

"Marching in the procession" was a very big deal for Adrienne, Marilou and Mimi. Tarted up in their frilliest springtime pastels, they'd traipse around the church wearing their best pious expressions and carefully tearing off pieces of their colonial bouquets to strew over the floor. Before the procession started, all the children and their mothers were kept in a holding pen off the nave of the church to await the signal to "march". One little boy held a single calla lily, but that year the wait was so long that by the time the procession started, he'd eaten it. The cousins loftily sniffed their disapproval.

Getting a new "Easter outfit" was a tradition observed at the time, place and station of our upbringing, and one to which we looked forward. Since Adrienne, Marilou and Mimi were so close in age to one another, someone in the family seized upon the notion of dressing them alike. It was probably Daddy. Any time he had the three girls together, he would inevitably be asked if they were triplets, and he always lied and said yes.

At the time, it was popular to deck out one's children in matching clothes. In our cases, it extended past sisters to include cousins. We have a photograph taken of Adrienne, Marilou and Mimi at age five in the Skyway restaurant of the Peabody Hotel, all three wearing the same plaid skirts, red jackets and little red beanies adorned with white pom-poms. Michele, identically attired, was not pictured as she was outside with Mother having a tantrum at the time.

Michele and Adrienne had already held a preview of their new glad rags for the benefit of the neighbors and the people in the cars speeding down Poplar. We'd sneaked out of the house one afternoon and made our way around the block, preening and strutting. When we eventually returned home, our first sight of the house included one of Mother standing on the front porch, arms akimbo, angrily gesturing us in. Corporal punishment was encouraged in those days.

We always got new Mary Janes for Easter. The style never varied; only the colors did. Black was obligatory for winter and white was considered proper for summer, with black patent considered a good default setting at any time. Rarely, one of the cousins would coax her mother into buying navy blue shoes or—be still, my heart—red ones, provoking fits of jealousy in the others.

Adding to the fun of shoe-shopping in 1940's Memphis were the X-ray machines which were standard equipment in all the stores, and which were used to check the fit of the shoes being considered. We didn't need a machine to tell us that a shoe hurt, but pretended otherwise so that we could look through the viewer and watch the bones of our toes dance around as we wiggled them. The object was to try on as many shoes as possible, with each new pair requiring an inspection.

That these devices emitted actual radiation didn't seem to concern anybody until the early '50's, and by 1960 they had been completely phased out. We've always wondered about the long-term effects of that radiation on the salespeople who operated them all day long.

With everyone appropriately dressed and shod, the entire clan would gather for Easter dinner, which exhibited more variety than did the other family holidays. Daddy might take a pork shoulder over to Leonard's, considered THE place to go for barbecue, where it would be smoked over live coals overnight in the pit that Leonard maintained. We still dream about the ravioli with the most wonderful Bolognese sauce that we hoped Aunt Leeze would bring from Barzizza's.

When we were younger, there would be Easter egg hunts held after dinner. Added to the usual cast of characters would be all of our Weber cousins, some of our second cousins, various schoolmates and the children of family friends. Prizes were awarded to the child finding the most eggs, and there was a $5 bill waiting for the one who found the "golden egg".

In preparation for these free-for-alls, Daddy and Mother, nominally assisted by Adrienne and Michele, would spend Easter Saturday night dying twelve dozen eggs. Mother always dyed the golden egg. She never managed to turn it gold, but its very peculiar color ensured that there would be no mistaking it when the prizes were handed out.

One Easter, four-year-old Bill Rowe had spotted an egg hidden under the concrete bench in the front yard. He'd cracked it open, eaten part of it, and thrown the rest under the concealing branches of the old evergreen. At the conclusion of the hunt, it became apparent that nobody'd found the Golden Egg, and everyone went back out to chase it down. When Bill saw Daddy looking under the bench, he realized that his snack had been the missing Golden Egg, but kept mum for fear of unpleasant consequences. After Marilou spotted the egg's remains under the evergreen, he felt that his desecration had been exposed and admitted to being the culprit. He still remembers his surprise and gratitude that instead of chastising him, Daddy gave him the $5 prize.

On Easter Sunday, while Mother and Daddy were outdoors hiding the eggs, the aunts and uncles herded all of us potential cheaters into the dining room and closed the drapes. The older ones of us were taken aside and told that if an egg was in plain sight, we were to leave it for a younger child. We would nod dutifully, with no intention whatever of allowing any of those mendacious brats to have an edge.

When all the guests were finally assembled, Daddy would open the door and yell, "GO!" A mad scramble would ensue. The veterans were familiar with Mother's and Daddy's favorite spots: the yucca, the hydrangeas, the rosebushes, under leaves at the bases of the trees, buried in the ivy, next to the swing supports, in the barbecue ovens, at the fence posts, in the drainpipes. Fights would erupt as two kids went for the same egg. Somebody would trip and fall, eggs would spill, and a few of them would be promptly scooped up by a competitor. The adults genuinely tried to supervise, but there were too many of us moving too fast for them to make much of a dint. Besides, they usually had their hands full with the weepers and wailers.

Next on the program were the games: the ever-popular relay race that involved running while carrying an egg on a spoon; the three-legged race, which was dropped from the roster when its danger to life and limb became evident.

After a few consecutive years of this bedlam, the grown-ups decided they'd had enough, and the egg hunts were no more. However, we did organize a few on our own for the benefit of our younger brothers and sisters, which represented a sharp departure from the contempt in which we held them when the stakes were higher.

On one of these occasions, two-year-old Justin turned up missing. A search party fanned out into the surrounding neighborhood, with everyone frantic. After about an hour, Paw-Paw found him, and there was general relief when they appeared hand-in-hand. Justin, ever curious, had simply gotten bored and wandered off. At least he was dressed. As toddlers, Kevitt and Chris were the original streakers, each taking advantage of any opportunity to take off running down the street naked as a jaybird.

The Easter when Michele was ten wasn't a happy one. She'd had an emergency appendectomy two weeks earlier, but hadn't made the expected recovery. By Easter morning, she was running a fever and was in considerable pain. Daddy and Mother took her to Baptist Hospital's emergency room, where the surgeon met them. Michele had developed an abscess, which required a second operation. Thus it was that Michele's appendectomy joined Aunt Leeze's thyroidectomy and Nana's hernia repair to complete a Grand Trine of ill-starred family surgeries.

THE MUSIC OF POPLAR STREET

In the Poplar Street living room hung a picture of St. Cecilia, the Catholic patron saint of music. The picture was large, probably three feet wide by four feet high. St. Cecilia's face bore an expression of pained resignation similar to that of most of the saints depicted in the religious artwork to which we were exposed as children. She was gazing heavenward, with one hand lightly placed on a piano, and the other raised as though reaching out imploringly to a vision.

Standing next to St. Cecilia were two burr-headed angels holding some sheet music. While most angels in the icons and holy cards of the day looked pious, these two seemed vaguely annoyed. We surmised that the music they were to sing did not appeal to them, and that their barely contained resentment was the cause of St. Cecilia's celestial weariness. In any event, we identified as much with the angels as with St. Cecilia.

Beneath the portrait of St. Cecilia was the piano Nana used to practice her scales. Nana was the principal soloist with St. Peter's choir, and we still remember her renditions of the technically challenging Bach-Gounod *Ave Maria*. Family folklore has it that she had once been invited to audition for the Metropolitan Opera.

One product of her diligent practice was that you could hear her sneeze in the next county. "Big lungs," she would always say to those of us who had taken cover.

To the amazed delight of those attending the Adler family reunion in 2002, Bill Rowe produced a tape recording of one of Nana's performances that his mother, Aunt Dokey, had given him. Most of us had never heard it, and the richness of her voice, even on the aged tape, was stunning. It was ironic that we were all dining at a restaurant that had once been a church: even in death, Nana managed to perform as a church soloist to a standing-room-only crowd.

There is a marvelous story connected with Nana's singing at St. Peter's that's still called the Christmas Miracle by Uncle Jack's family. It was related to us several years ago by our cousin John, Uncle Jack's son.

During the Depression, Uncle Jack had been living in Washington, D.C. while attending law school at Georgetown University. It was Christmas Eve, and the family fortunes were such that his parents couldn't afford to bring him home to Memphis for Christmas. He had gone to a movie downtown, then returned to his room, feeling pretty low. He turned on the radio, and found a station that was playing some beautiful Christmas music.

In times past, it was common on Christmas Eve for radio stations to broadcast church celebrations from all over the country. Suddenly, Uncle Jack realized that he was listening to a live broadcast of Midnight Mass at St. Peter's in Memphis, and that the soloist was his own mother.

In our family, coincidences that are not coincidences frequently involve music.

In 1985, Michele was attending Mass on Father's Day at a Catholic church in Tampa, Florida. As she looked around the church at all the dads there with their families, she began thinking of Daddy. She was lost in thought, remembering his irreverent approach to life, his occasional naivete, and his deep love for his children. Meanwhile, the Mass had ended, and the organist was playing the recessional hymn.

Nowadays, the music played in Catholic churches is almost always liturgical music; secular music is heard rarely, if ever. So Michele was totally stunned when she realized that not only was secular music being played, but it was *The Triumphal March* from the opera *Aida*.

The Triumphal March was one of Daddy's favorites, so much so that he insisted it be played instead of the Mendelssohn wedding march when he married Mother in 1940. Though *Aida* has enjoyed a revival in recent years, in 1985 productions were few and far between, and the odds that a random church organist would be both familiar with the *March* and capable of playing it were quite long. The odds that Michele would have been in that church on Father's Day to hear that music being played are astronomical.

In June of 2008, we experienced a third occurrence of this phenomenon. Jeremy Adler, the oldest of Chris and Susan's three children, was the first of our parents' grandchildren to marry. His wedding to his bride Elizabeth Dees was being held in Mobile, Alabama, and we had just arrived to join in the celebration of the occasion. We were struggling to get our luggage into the hotel room we would share.

Though both of us have traveled extensively, we've never checked into a hotel room where the television was not only on, but tuned to the music channel. As we entered the room and set down our luggage, Adrienne realized that the music being played was the *Intermezzo* from *Cavalleria Rusticano*. Again, it had been another favorite of Daddy's, one that we'd had played at his funeral. We told Susan, Jeremy's mother, that we felt Daddy was sending a blessing to Jeremy and Elizabeth in the best way he knew how.

Perhaps these events weren't that coincidental after all, since music provides a running thread that connects the generations in our family. It has been a major part of our lives, and we learned to love it at early ages.

Mother would take Adrienne for walks around the block when she was a toddler, and each day they would pass a house on Bellevue Street that belonged to a music teacher. One day, Mother heard piano music coming from the house, and on impulse went up and rang the doorbell. The teacher answered, and the end result was that Mother signed four-year-old Adrienne up for lessons.

It was soon apparent to Nana that Adrienne had a real aptitude for the instrument. Nana asked her friends in Memphis music circles to recommend a teacher of more advanced knowledge and skills, and settled on one at Southwestern (now Rhodes) College of Music's preparatory department. Thus began Adrienne's studies with Ialeen Dunning, which lasted through her senior year in high school. It was at Southwestern that it was discovered that Adrienne had been gifted with absolute pitch, the ability to name or reproduce musical tones without referring to any other external source.

Later, Mother saw to it that Michele received piano lessons also. Michele claims that the only reason for this was to keep her from indulging in accusatory griping later.

Mother also introduced Michele to the ukelele, probably with the whimsical hope that her daughter would be asked to play on Arthur Godfrey's show, which Mother greatly admired. Michele, who had no desire to migrate to the islands OR to New York, blew off the lessons.

Though Nana only occasionally practiced her scales on it, the old Kimball piano did yeoman work for years. It was the instrument that Adrienne used from her first hesitant plinks to the virtuosity she later came to display.

Michele had her own star turn, which she initially piggy-backed onto Adrienne's. One of the first pieces that Adrienne played was a nursery-room dazzler called *Little Bear, Wake Up,* which ended dramatically with a single high C. Michele, at age two, would listen attentively and knew when this grand finale was approaching. Just in time for it, she would run to the piano, hit the highest note on the keyboard, and squeal "Ping!" Adrienne was not amused that her thunder had been stolen.

As children, we wondered why Mother and Daddy had as few friends as they did. It hadn't yet occurred to us that it might have been because anyone invited to Poplar Street was frog-marched into watching us perform. First, Adrienne would blunder through her latest piano assignment. Then, Michele would come onstage in full cowgirl attire to render a rousing version of "I Didn't Know the Gun Was Loaded", a hit song which Mother first heard on Arthur Godfrey's program.

In her college and medical school years, Adrienne would treat the family to midnight recitals when she came home from a date that Had Not Gone Well. The piano was located in the foyer at that time, allowing melancholy strains of Chopin, Lizst and/or Debussy to float through the house as the drama queen melodically telegraphed that the date had bombed.

Both of us won various talent shows throughout our childhood; Adrienne for piano, Michele for singing. Additionally, we would perform in the solo recitals that were expected of students enrolled in Southwestern's Preparatory department, and occasionally we'd team up. Whatever the case, receptions at Poplar Street were de rigeur after these events, as Daddy thought that the house count would be greatly enhanced if the audience could anticipate restorative cocktails later.

The last of these receptions was the one that followed Adrienne's senior recital in 1958, which achieved legendary status in the annals of Poplar Street.

Southwestern's College of Music was housed in a beautiful old antebellum mansion on Overton Park Avenue, surrounded by a full city block of land. Daddy would stand outside as the guests arrived, effusively welcoming the "music lovers". These had always included family, friends of the family and teachers, but the guest list had been expanded that final year.

Adrienne and her friends were all dating boys who were freshmen at Christian Brothers College, at the time an exclusively male institution. All the boys had been invited to the concert, and not a one of them planned to attend—until word got out about the nature of the reception that was to follow. They showed up en masse.

Adrienne was already on CBC's list of potential subversives because of the Brothers' embarrassed discovery that she'd been only fourteen years old when the college's student body elected her to be their first homecoming queen two years earlier. At that time, any girl who could cajole one of the boys into submitting her picture was eligible.

In a burst of irony, it was one of the nuns at Sacred Heart, affectionately known as CJ, who was responsible for getting Adrienne nominated. CJ was very popular both with the girls at Sacred Heart and with their brothers and boyfriends. "Mike," as we shall call the young man, who put Adrienne's name in the pot, had just broken up with his girlfriend; she was now dating another guy in his class. The new flame had already proposed her for queen, and Mike asked CJ if she knew of a girl who might also be a contender. CJ suggested Adrienne, a sophomore at the time but younger than the rest because of having skipped third grade. Mike was unconcerned about her age, which he recorded as sixteen on the application.

To the surprise of one and all, Adrienne was one of four finalists, which included Mike's ex. The four were paraded in front of an assembly of the cat-calling students, who then voted. Since this was 1956, the girls were under no compunction to be committed to saving the whales in Afghanistan or to otherwise pretend to a non-existent humanitarianism, and Adrienne—and most especially Mike—emerged victorious.

Though the Christian Brothers subsequently stipulated that candidates for the honor be college students, they remained stuck with the fact that Adrienne, their first queen, conjured up visions of Lolita.

The reception following the piano recital only enhanced her dubious legend. The damage probably could have been contained had it not happened that CBC was holding an event that night in which most of the young men attending the afternoon recital were expected to participate.

The concert ended around four o'clock, and the largest audience ever to attend a Preparatory School function swarmed over Poplar Street. The house was packed with people of all ages, and no one was in charge of crowd control as Daddy made certain that the hospitality flowed to one and all. He conveniently dismissed the legalities of the situation, rationalizing that these applied to public establishments, not to private homes—and never, of course, to Poplar Street.

The results were predictable. They were also patently obvious when the partygoers showed up at CBC for the scheduled event in less than presentable condition.

The Christian Brothers were understandably livid. The following day, the college president called the nun who was the principal of Sacred Heart and gave her an earful in which the words "homecoming queen" were no doubt given some prominence. Sister promptly passed both his sentiments and her own on to Daddy, who regrettably responded according to his operating premise that the best defense is a good offense.

Mother, it should be said, had done her passive-aggressive best to convince Adrienne and Daddy to limit the underage guests to family and close girlfriends. Nana, for once, agreed with her. For years later, Mother would opine, "Once Adrienne and her daddy got an idea, you couldn't stop them." It should be noted that not all of our elders needed adult supervision. It was just Daddy who did.

Six weeks later, Adrienne graduated second in her class. Daddy was convinced that she was denied first honors because of the party, though Adrienne assured him that the valedictorian had won it fair and square. He refused to believe her; characteristically, he also showed no remorse about presiding over the party in the first place. That fall, Michele, Kevitt and Chris were enrolled at Immaculate Conception, and Sacred Heart School remained on Daddy's blacklist until the day it closed.

Carol Rowe only recently told us of a rumor that she'd heard many years ago, to the effect that the upstanding young men of CBC had been forbidden to darken the door of 1234 Poplar, which the Brothers had presumably come to regard as a den of iniquity. Carol had been dating someone who was in school there, and as they drove past Poplar Street she mentioned that this was where her grandparents lived. Her date then proceeded to inform her that the CBC students had all been told that the Poplar Street house was off limits. If this was indeed the case, the Christian Brothers would have had the last laugh when the house which they banned because of the drinking that took place there became a detention facility for alcohol and drug offenders.

However, Poplar Street as we knew it existed in a different day and a different time, when blaming the bartender was akin to shooting the messenger: Excessive drinking was held to be an individual moral and/ or social failing that could be overcome with enough will power. Though the large body of knowledge that exists today on the subject has generally dispelled this view, Daddy's insistence that "it wasn't my fault if those boys couldn't hold their liquor!" was in keeping with his own zeitgeist—though still leaving him a heavy favorite to win the Bad Judgment Sweepstakes.

LAMB OF GOD

The musical gene replicating itself within the family finally emerged to command an international stage courtesy of Jim Adler, who literally fathered the heavy metal band *Lamb of God* via his sons, Chris and Will Adler. Chris, who launched the group, is widely recognized as being the leading heavy metal drummer in the world; he has also authored and published a book entitled *Lamb of God: New American Gospel*. Will is a top guitarist and a creative artist who has written much of the original music that the band has performed.

When *Lamb of God* received its second Grammy nomination in 2010, Jim was invited to attend the event and had gone to Los Angeles several days in advance of it. Jim, who could create a party atmosphere at a wake, was having himself a grand old time when he received a call from Chris and Will: they'd been stranded in Richmond by a snowstorm. They informed Jim that there was no way they could get to LA in time for the Grammys, and that he was going to have to accept the award for them should they win. They assured him that people from Sony, the parent company of their label, Epic Records, would be on hand to shepherd him through the process.

So it was that Jim's niece, Kerry Adler, was watching a live stream of the Grammys on her computer in hopes of getting a glimpse of her cousins.

Suddenly, she was heard to yell, "OMIGOD! It's Uncle Jim! On the Red Carpet!"

Sure enough, there was Jim, parading around as though to the manner born.

At the after-party hosted by Sony, he found himself seated between Elton John and Tony Bennett. Though *Lamb of God* had lost to another group, the words that Tony Bennett spoke to Jim will remain forever etched on his heart: "You're the oldest heavy-metal fan I've ever met!"

PART FOUR

POPLAR STREET AND THE RITES OF PASSAGE

Weddings and Engagements

Including how Adrienne married Jim on three days' notice

The Poplar Street Way of Death

Poplar Street Underground

Epilogue

WEDDINGS AND ENGAGEMENTS

It had become a Poplar Street tradition to hold pre-wedding parties in honor of the impending marriages within the family. Diane and Kevitt were feted with the usual Poplar Street gala the night before their wedding, only in this instance the party served as Mother's and Daddy's version of a rehearsal dinner.

On that day, November 25, 1969, Memphis was holding one of its periodic voter referendums on whether or not to permit liquor to be served by the drink in public establishments. As the matter stood, a restaurant or bar could not serve alcoholic drinks. Customers who wanted them had to bring in their own liquor, and could rely upon the establishment to provide only ice, glasses, and mixers. The customers then had to assemble their own libations. Obviously, this meant that many people whose alcohol intake might have been constrained by the price of multiple drinks on their beverage tabs were happily putting away entire bottles.

In past elections, the proposal had been voted down thanks to an unlikely coalition of the liquor store owners and the Protestant ministers. Though normally crossing swords, the two warring factions called a truce every few years when they teamed up to defeat a measure that threatened both of their core businesses. The liquor store owners feared losing their pub-crawling clientele, and the ministers feared that congregants who wouldn't dream of buying a bottle of booze might not be so squeamish if it were a matter of only a drink or two.

Conveniently for the good citizens of 1234 Poplar, the polls were located directly across the street at what was then Tech High School. It had been a busy day for Michele, and she hadn't yet voted. Dressed in an evening gown in anticipation of the festivities, she decided that since she had a few minutes before the guests were to arrive, she'd make a quick dash over to Tech and perform her Civic Duty. She was relieved to see that the line was short as she leaned over to sign the registration book, realizing too late that her décolletage was very much on display. As she was leaving, she was taken aback to hear someone sneer, "Well! I guess we know how SHE voted!"

Back at Poplar Street, the party was in full swing. Monsignor Merlin Kearney, who was to officiate at the wedding, had been extended an invitation, and to everyone's surprise had actually shown up. There he was, enthusiastically if not brilliantly pounding the keyboard of the old Kimball piano.

Monsignor Kearney, known to the more irreverent among us as "Big Mon", was an outgoing, flamboyant sort who would have probably been just as comfortable

operating as a ward heeler as he was in the priesthood.
When the funeral train carrying the remains of Robert F. Kennedy arrived at Washington D.C.'s Union
Station, Michele, who was watching the proceedings
on television, was startled to spot Monsignor Kearney
among the disembarking mourners.

Monsignor had ingratiated himself with the Adlers
when they'd moved to Court Street and hence into
Sacred Heart parish, where he was a recently ordained
priest on one of his first assignments. The relationship waxed and waned from that time forward. Daddy
would tell of driving young Father Kearney around
town at the age of ten, when no one cared about such
niceties as drivers' licenses or whether children were
at the wheel. Daddy also affectionately recalled riding
Father's dog, the first in a series of St. Bernards that he
would own over the next fifty years.

After Father became Monsignor Kearney and was
made pastor of Immaculate Conception Church, he had
a large pen built next to the rectory to accommodate
his beloved pets. The huge dogs would bark constantly
and fearsomely at the parishioners attending Sunday
Mass, who had to pass by the pen on their way from the
parking lot to the church.

Brides and bridesmaids who elected to dress at the
church for weddings there were given the use of a room
in the rectory which sported a white bearskin rug and
a floor-to-ceiling portrait of Monsignor with the Pope.
Adrienne, one of Marilou's bridesmaids, burst into the
room on the morning of the wedding, late and nursing

a headache. Unaware of the existence of the portrait, she initially thought she might be hallucinating.

Adrienne's infirmities that morning were minor.

Marilou's wedding had been preceded the night before by the usual Poplar Street blowout, after which Adrienne, Ann Chaney and their dates had gone elsewhere to continue the party. Returning to Poplar Street at 2:00 a.m, Adrienne was startled to realize that the dark splotches she kept encountering on the way up the stairs were bloodstains. She woke Michele to get the full story: It seemed that Justin and Chris were playing Superman, which involved jumping off the top of the large armoire in Chris's bedroom. Justin missed the bed on one of his leaps, and instead struck some immovable object that opened up an inch or two of his scalp. This effectively ended the party, as the parents of the bride were obliged to cart their son off to the emergency room for multiple sutures.

Justin, swathed in bandages, would have his momentary lapse of concentration forever immortalized in the wedding pictures.

WEDDINGS

Poplar Street was also pressed into service for several family wedding receptions, including those held when Chris married Susan Morris in 1978 and when our cousin Ann Chaney married Don Gillespie in 1968. These receptions seemed to fit on a sliding scale between Aunt Dokey's, the first one, which saw every i dotted and every t crossed, and Adrienne's, which blatantly disregarded every tradition except the use of the cutwork tablecloth.

AUNT DOKEY AND UNCLE MARINE

On April 20, 1940, the society pages of the Memphis Commercial Appeal carried a lengthy piece headlined, "Miss Dorothea Cecile Adler Will Be Wed this Morning", heralding the wedding of Aunt Dokey to Uncle Marine Rowe. They'd had a long courtship following their meeting at a college dance one Halloween, allowing Uncle Marine to joke forever after that "the witches got hold of him that night!" And when he told her during the course of their first conversation that his own birthday, like hers, was on January 22nd, she thought it was a pick-up line. Naturally, these tidbits were not included in the newspaper article.

What WAS included was an exquisitely detailed description of the bride's ivory slipper satin gown embroidered with seed pearls, her French illusion double-tiered veil extending to the end of her train, the multihued pastel silk net dresses with matching hats worn by her six attendants, the profusion of blossoms and greenery adorning the altar and sanctuary of St. Peter's Church and the elaborate bouquets carried by bride and bridesmaids.

Nana's fine hand was obvious in the musical program. In addition to the customary Panis Angelicus and Ave Maria, it included selections by Wagner,

Debussy, and Liszt performed by Arthur Hays, the choirmaster and organist at St. Peter's, and Elsa Gerber, one of the few sopranos in Memphis whose talents met with Nana's approval.

Aunt Ding was her cousin's maid of honor, and the wedding party also included Aunt Leeze, Uncle Dut, Uncle Jack and Daddy.

Afterward, everyone adjourned to Poplar Street, which apparently had been spit-polished to a mirror shine. To quote the article:

> *Following the ceremony, Mr. and Mrs. Adler will entertain with a reception for members of the bridal party, the immediate families and out-of-town guests.*
>
> *An all-white bridal motif with accents of green will be carried out in decorations   of the reception rooms. Vases of Easter lilies, snapdragons, stock and other spring flowers will be used.*
>
> *The bride's table, draped with a Roman cutwork cloth of Cluny medallions with a filet lace edge, will be centered with a tiered wedding cake, garlanded with crystal links filled with valley lilies. Tall white candles will burn at each side.*
>
> *Mrs. Adler, receiving with Mr. Adler, will be gowned in a model of Madonna blue with a sweetheart neckline. The bodice features the new*

band puffing and the skirt   is flared. She will wear
hat and gloves of matching color......"

The menu featured chicken a la king, considered the very embodiment of gourmet cuisine at the time. Twenty-five years later, Nana was still fuming over the guest who informed her that it was so good she'd had five plates of it. "The nerve of her! And to think she never even sent a gift!"

ADRIENNE AND JIM

Adrienne and Jim got married on three days' notice. Adrienne was interning at George Washington University Hospital in Washington, D.C. at the time, and was looking forward to a ten-day vacation that was just beginning on that Friday, December 2. She and Jim had met in late August on a blind date arranged by a colleague of Adrienne's who'd been Jim's fraternity brother in college. He'd told Adrienne that he wanted her to meet his friend because "you're the only female I've ever known who's as off the wall as he is."

They met and they clicked.

Adrienne introduced Jim to the rest of the family on a weekend in early November when she had two days off from work. She'd been talking about her family and friends in Memphis, and Jim had said, "Let's go see them." He picked up the phone and booked a flight that departed an hour later. Adrienne called home and arranged for someone to pick them up when they arrived in Memphis at 1:00 a.m., and off they went.

The family decided they vastly preferred Jim to Adrienne. During their visit, Jim stopped and picked up a bouquet of roses for Mother, something nobody, not even Daddy, had ever done for her. At that point, she was Jim's for life. She sidled up to Adrienne later that day and let her know that "I'd sure like to have him for a son-in-law!" A month later, her wish came true.

Jim and Adrienne had been sitting around their favorite bar, the cocktail lounge at Washington's Madison Hotel, planning what they were going to do during the ten days that Adrienne was free. They'd already decided they'd marry, and it was just a question of when. They began discussing time frames, and after several scotches it became apparent that the best time to do it was...right now!

Adrienne called Michele and told her that she and Jim were getting married, but to keep quiet about it for the moment. She asked Michele to find out if there was 1) any waiting period before being granted a marriage license in Memphis, and 2) how long it took to get the blood test for syphilis which was required at the time. Michele did some digging, and got back to them with the news that there was no waiting period if the parties were over 21, which they were, and that a blood test could be obtained in a matter of hours if one had connections, which Adrienne did.

With this information in hand, Adrienne called Daddy on Saturday morning.

"Daddy! Guess what! I'm getting married!"

"Ohshit...."

"To Jim. This week. At Sacred Heart. You have to fix it."

Daddy went like a homing pigeon to the only priest in the diocese who had the authority to waive the "banns". These were the public announcements of an engagement that had to be made for three consecutive weeks from the pulpit of the church where the couple was to marry, thus giving the congregation time to dig up any dirt that might render the upcoming marriage invalid. By this time, Sacred Heart School had closed, and the diocese had relocated its offices to the former school building. The chancellor of the diocese also served at Sacred Heart Church, and it was he to whom Daddy went.

Daddy called Adrienne back later that afternoon. "Wednesday morning at 9:00," he told her.

"We'll be there!"

Adrienne flew to Memphis on Sunday night. Her first order of business on Monday was to find a dress, since Mother had adamantly refused to make one for her. She and Michele went to Levy's, one of Memphis's most exclusive purveyors of fine clothing. They stepped off the elevator and into the hushed, thickly carpeted inner sanctum of the store's designer salon, where bridal attire was sold. An elegantly dressed and coiffed saleslady greeted the two interlopers.

"How may I assist you?" she inquired, looking down at them through her pince-nez glasses.

"I'm getting married, and I need a dress", chirped Adrienne.

The saleslady beamed approval. "And when is the wedding?" she cooed.

"The day after tomorrow. We just decided to do it, so we're keeping it informal. I was thinking of a suit..."

Like most of her colleagues at Levy's, this lady was the epitome of vintage Memphis propriety. Her glasses were sliding progressively farther down her nose as Adrienne prattled away. "And what size do you wear?"

"I'm not sure. You see, I've gained a little weight, and......"

Michele barely suppressed a groan as the glasses fell off the saleslady's face. As the woman readjusted her eyewear and stalked imperiously through the French doors hiding the racks of dresses, Michele hissed at Adrienne, "Good grief, she thinks this is a shotgun wedding and that you're pregnant!"

The saleslady, having recovered her poise, sailed back into view bearing a white silk suit. Adrienne tried it on, found that it fit, and bought it. They'd been in and out of the store in less than half an hour, to Michele's immense relief. She kept muttering to Adrienne all the way home that there were times when she felt like the person who walked behind the circus elephant with a shovel.

Back at Poplar Street, chaos reigned. Mother was busily planning the reception, but on further investigation it appeared that she was planning it for the night before, not the day of, the wedding. The only explanation was that she'd planned so many big parties for the nights before family weddings that she must have just assumed in her rattled state that this was what she was supposed to do.

Fortunately, Jim got into town shortly afterward and began organizing things. As various aunts and cousins showed up, he'd assign them jobs. "Aunt Leeze, you're the food committee", he told her as she walked in the door. Behind her was Aunt Ding, who'd just come in from Dallas. Jim informed her that she was the flower committee. "We'll need bouquets for Adrienne and Michele, an arrangement on the altar and something for the dining room table. Go!" They scurried off.

It stands to reason that the more time that's available to plan a spur-of-the-moment wedding, the more time there is to think up flourishes that aren't possible on the spur-of-the-moment. Having failed in her harebrained attempt to talk Mother into making her dress, Adrienne then glommed onto the notion of having the

Triumphal March from Aida played as a recessional, just as Mother and Daddy had done at their wedding in 1940. Naturally, no one in Memphis could accommodate her on such short notice, so Adrienne decided that she'd record it herself and have the recording played at the wedding. Mercifully, Sacred Heart wasn't equipped to handle this, so Adrienne very reluctantly dropped the idea. That was when Jim appointed a music committee.

He also appointed a liquor committee, a transportation committee and whatever committee came to mind if he saw anyone standing idle. An emergency housecleaning was in progress. Silver was being polished, and table linens were being aired out and ironed after their long confinement in the bottom drawer of the buffet. Daddy hired some of his packing house employees to help serve at the reception, temporarily relieving them of their usual jobs which might have had something to do with bovine entrails.

That evening, Jim's parents, Dick and Kay, and two of his sisters arrived. His sister Judy was carrying her three-month old son, Mike, who was born the day that Jim and Adrienne met. Joining them for the flight to Memphis were two of Jim's friends, Paul and Jerry. Paul had become greatly interested in learning to play the harmonica, for which he had no aptitude whatsoever. Unconcerned about his woeful lack of talent, he played the only tune he'd mastered, which was *Red River Valley*, constantly.

Once on board the plane, Paul had Jerry convince the flight attendant that there was a concert harmonica player on board, who would graciously consent to entertain the passengers with his music if he were asked. The next thing Dick and Kay knew, the flight attendant was announcing that they were in for a rare treat, and went on to introduce Paul. Over the intercom came the now-painfully familiar strains of *Red River Valley*. Judy vowed then and there to steal the harmonica and hide it in Mike's diaper bag for the return flight.

The wedding party—such as it was—stopped by Sacred Heart Church on Tuesday evening to formulate a game plan for the wedding. It wasn't a "rehearsal" as most people understand it.

The priest perfunctorily asked, "And will you want to make your confession before you receive the sacrament of Matrimony?"

"Yes," answered Jim. "Bring your lunch."

Jim, along with other out-of-town guests, had booked a room at the nearby Admiral Benbow Inn. After a meet-and-greet at Poplar Street, during which the families of the bride and groom got to either allay or reinforce their suspicions about each other, Jim had decided to go back to the Inn and get some sleep.

Jerry and Paul had been joined by Walt, another friend of Jim's, and the three of them were conspiring to dissuade Jim from his planned Health Night. When this proved futile, Jerry decided that if nothing else was to come of the evening, the least he could do was to procure a souvenir.

Projecting from the Admiral Benbow's façade were several long flagpoles, from which large flags flapped over the traffic hurtling down Union Avenue. When John Adler arrived later that evening, the staff at the Inn was in an uproar about some jackass who'd been trying to shimmy out on a flagpole and steal one of the flags. John, instantly recognizing that the prank was somehow related to the upcoming wedding, beat a quick retreat to his room and stayed there.

Jim and Adrienne were married the next morning, December 7, 1966. They were gratified by the number of friends and family, many from out-of-town, who'd dropped everything to come. Michele was Adrienne's maid-of-honor, and Kevitt was Jim's best man. Adrienne detoured after the ceremony and put her bridal bouquet at the church's separate altar to Our Lady of Perpetual Help. It must have been deeply appreciated by Mother that the preferred icon of the Floating Blood Clot Novenas would be so honored.

All of the committees performed admirably, though Uncle Dut, the photography committee, lost his shots inside the church due to poor lighting. It didn't matter, because his outdoor ones came out beautifully, and provided the only pictorial record that Adrienne and Jim would ever have of their wedding.

At the reception, Paul led off a toast to the newlyweds with a large gulp of the straight scotch that he was drinking from Mother's sterling silver pitcher. Later, Jerry and Walt organized a touch football game on the grounds of William R. Moore School next door. At one point, the football landed on the flat roof of the school, which posed a problem since it was the only ball they had.

Jerry sprang into action. He climbed up the metal struts supporting the sawdust vent and jumped onto the roof, where he retrieved the ball. Then, he spotted an open window dead ahead and climbed through it. He was startled to land in a room where a class was in progress; the students and the teacher were equally startled to see an apparition wearing dress clothes and clutching a football. Jerry obsequiously murmured his apologies as he backed toward the door and made his escape.

But the most indelible impression of Adrienne's and Jim's wedding was formed at the end of the Mass that followed the ceremony, when the organist struck up the recessional march. Plainly audible above the crashing chords of the organ was the sound of a harmonica playing *Red River Valley*. Badly.

THE POPLAR STREET WAY OF DEATH

There is an old superstition which holds that when you see three ravens on the roof of a house, it means someone will die in the house within the week.

We never needed such silliness. We had relatives who could sense death, were fascinated by it, and liked to be of service to it. Whenever a family member was in dire straits, inquiries were made as to whether any of the Specters at the Feast had come to call.

If the answer was yes, it was accepted that the aforementioned family member probably had less than a week. No one knew exactly what they knew or how they knew it. They just showed up without notification, and sat with the about-to-be-departed.

These special family members—and they were special—had very firm views about funeral protocol. The coffin had to be open. The corpse had to look its best. They may have had a rating system for the latter: Nana's corpse, for example, seemed to win hands down when one observed that "Baby looks so purty lying there in her coffin!"

So Daddy's funeral threw some of them for a loop. Given his very recent brain surgery, we had decided to keep the coffin closed despite cries that "This is the first Adler funeral where the coffin hasn't been open!" Since you don't antagonize people who can replace ravens on the roof, we compromised. We agreed that they could view Daddy while we waited outside, because we just couldn't handle it.

Some of the group specialized. One relative excelled in celebrating the completed passage to the other side. Though she could have earned a comfortable living as a professional mourner, we received her services gratis. No family funeral was complete without her sympathy histrionics.

Whenever you heard "WAAAHAAAHAAA-HOOO!!" at a funeral, you knew she was somewhere among the mourners. Her cries resounded through the church, punctuating the Panis Angelicus and the Ave Maria that were the musical staples of any Adler funeral. Any little ones in attendance would be so entranced by the spectacle that they'd forget to whine. She was better than a baby-sitter.

Clearly, the Poplar Street way of death needed an imprimatur, and the Specters were the closest thing we had. Which brings us to the Adler Mausoleum, built at a time when death actually had panache.

THE MAUSOLEUM

Back in 1916, Great-Grandpa Adler erected a solid marble mausoleum in the city's Calvary Cemetery. It was a six-seater, designed to hold himself, Great-Grandma Adler and their four children. One of these children had died in infancy, and he and Great-Grandma shared a slot.

After Paw-Paw parted ways with his sisters, he declared among other things that he would NOT be buried in the mausoleum. He pointed out that he'd wanted nothing to do with his siblings in life, and he sure as hell didn't want anything to do with them in death.

The mausoleum today serves primarily as a signpost guiding one to the family plot. A granite angel with wings unfurled stands poised atop the mausoleum, and following his line of sight allows one to chance across the graves.

These graves hold a lot of Adlers, but the Reedys, Nana's relatives, are also well represented. A closer look at the tombstones reveals that early summer was a popular time for our forebears to give up the ghost. "If this family can get through the last week of June and the first week of July, we'll be fine for the rest of the year," Aunt Dokey once said. It was true. Paw-Paw and Nana both died in that time frame. And Daddy and Mother both died on July 6th, though 18 years apart.

Why? Who knows? We've speculated that it may have something to do with Memphis being one of the hottest places on earth during that time of year, and with God deciding that throwing all of us into the infernal heat of Calvary Cemetery to bury somebody was a fitting penance for our sins. It's as good of an explanation as any.

POPLAR STREET FUNERAL GATHERINGS

Poplar Street was a great venue for all sorts of gatherings, and served the family well when one of its members died. After the funeral, the mourners would repair to Poplar Street to share their memories of the recently departed and to restore themselves with large quantities of food and drink. Especially drink. Pretty soon, everybody forgot about the deceased and concentrated on making merry, a clear case of spirits conquering spirits.

The first funeral we ever attended followed the death of Uncle Duddy, when Adrienne and Michele were eight and five years old, respectively. Uncle Duddy had been Nana's brother. He was 70, and he'd never married. Since he lived in Chicago, our only contact with him had been on his rare visits, when Adrienne bitched mightily about having to "give up her room".

At the time of his death, Uncle Duddy was checked into a Chicago hotel. We children were told by our father that he'd "leaned out the window to get some air, and I guess he musta leaned over too far, because he fell out!" Actually, Daddy used the same line on the priest with whom he was attempting to make funeral arrangements. His version of events was obviously given the benefit of the doubt, because Uncle Duddy was dispatched with a Requiem Mass and burial in consecrated ground, privileges that were denied during that era to those who'd committed suicide.

Uncle Duddy had told some of the family a year earlier that he was going to shoot himself. He'd then produced a gun that he'd bought from Sears, and announced that this was the gun he was going to use to do it. Being a wonderfully dysfunctional little group, nobody paid a grain of attention to him.

After his death, his personal effects were sent back to Nana. Included was the gun, still unopened and in its original box. Nana promptly took it back to Sears and got credit for it. To this day, the story serves as a litmus test of a person's life view. People either erupt in peals of laughter or get odd looks on their faces and say, "Well, it had never been used…" The latter comment has been verifiably heard from only one person in the family: Daddy. We seem to remember Mark Downs, Adrienne's son, having the same reaction, but Mark denies it.

The main thing we remembered about Uncle Duddy's funeral was getting to ride in the limousine's jump seats. Though quite uncomfortable for anyone over the age of 8, these seats were prized by the younger children, who vied for the honor of occupying them.

Another relative passed away when we were in high school. Like most teenagers, we were susceptible to bouts of inappropriate laughter in situations where a solemn demeanor was not only expected but required. We succumbed to such a bout at the funeral service of this elderly family member. We had joined Marilou and Sherry at the funeral home, where the visitation was in progress. The four of us approached the casket and stood looking down at the deceased, trying not to cry at losing someone who'd been part of our lives ever since we could remember.

In his youth, our relative had sustained an injury that left a small indentation in his forehead. It had fascinated us as young children, and to satisfy our curiosity we had been told that a bullet had grazed his forehead during World War I. As we stood paying our respects, Marilou intoned in her most sonorous, funereal voice: "Y'all, look. He's still got that little hole in his head..."

Somebody stifled a snort of mirth, hoping it would sound like a choked sob, and that was all it took. With hands over our faces and shoulders shaking, we managed to make it outside before we scandalized everyone. Despite the sincerity of our grief, it was just one of those moments.

PALLBEARERS

Daddy died at 70, but many of his friends went before him. This meant that he'd had numerous requests to serve as a pallbearer. These experiences taught him that all pallbearers are not created equal. Rather than carrying their assigned loads, some would just hold onto the handle of the coffin, look reverent, and leave the heavy lifting to everyone else.

Daddy called these people "riders."

He would frequently come home from a funeral grousing that there'd been another rider among the pallbearers. His frustration was amplified because he didn't know the specific identity of the rider; he only knew that there WAS one, and that was good enough for him.

Then one fine funeral, the rider was the pallbearer directly across from him. At last, a verifiable culprit! Not only was there a rider, but it was a rider whose lazy ineptitude directly affected Daddy by making him shoulder the load for both of them. Outside the church, Dad was holding up the coffin with all his might, and seething. He leaned across the coffin with what strength he had left and snarled at the rider: "Why don't you just get on top of this thing, and we'll carry you, too!!"

The line lives on still. At every funeral we attend, we wonder if there's a "rider". Probably not, since the funeral homes, wary of litigation, now leave little actual work for the pallbearers to do. And pallbearers aren't needed to carry cremains.

At Daddy's funeral, a man whose name we didn't know came up to say how great Daddy was, but added, "You know, he got mad about things that weren't worth getting mad about." We speculated that he might have been one of the riders, which led us into wondering if any of the pallbearers carrying Daddy's own casket would turn out to be riders.

This was only one of many sources of comedic material that we mined for laughs at Daddy's funeral, because we knew that when we quit laughing we'd start crying.

After we picked out the coffin, the funeral director, who was straight out of Central Casting, informed us that we needed a vault to "seal" it.

Mother pondered this. "Why?" she asked. "Does it leak?"

Michele then spotted one that had the Good Housekeeping Seal of Approval affixed to it. She was fascinated.

"What do you do? Go out ten years later and dig it up to see if it's still meeting standards?"

We remembered that Daddy had always said he wanted to be buried face down, so that "all the people I've told to kiss my ass will have one last opportunity." Somebody got the idea of asking Lurch, as we'd named the funeral director, if this would be possible. Unfortunately, no one did, so we are minus one more great funeral memory: The Specters' reaction to a posthumous mooning.

The funeral director had reminded Mother that there were two remaining plots at Calvary, and wanted to know which one would be Daddy's. He explained that one of the plots was adjacent to Nana's grave.

Mother said simply, "Put him next to his Mama."

And so that is the lineup in Calvary today. The four north plots include Paw-Paw, Nana, Daddy, then Mother. In death as in life.

Poplar Street Underground.

Forever.

EPILOGUE

There was an afternoon ritual that occurred at any Poplar Street holiday celebration, be it Christmas, Thanksgiving or Easter. After the huge dinners, Paw-Paw would unceremoniously put on his hat and head for Poplar Street's front door, signaling to all the grandchildren that it was time for The Walk. All of us would scramble to accompany him—and then, to keep up with him.

The Walk involved enough of mid-town Memphis that we needed Paw-Paw's time-tested navigation skills to guide our steps. And shortly before we returned home, we would recognize the symbol that both The Walk and the holiday were drawing to a close.

We'd see the railroad tracks.

We were never sure how we got there, but we knew that home was near when we saw this mountain looming ahead, crowned by railroad tracks that were used daily by various trains for more mundane experiences. We all cheered and steeled ourselves for the thrill and the challenge of climbing over the tracks. Afterward, we'd triumphantly make our way back to Poplar Street in the light of a setting sun.

Then one Christmas, a few of us grew up.

We learned there was no "naughty or nice" list. We quit racing down the stairs on Christmas morning to see what Santa had left us, and started helping our parents set out the gifts for the younger ones. We even joined the "grown-ups" table for the holiday meals. And we noticed with sudden, shocking disappointment that the huge mountain where the railroad tracks ran was really just a little hill of no major importance. We wondered why we had made such a fuss about it.

We didn't go on any more walks with Paw-Paw.

We had passed the Christmas that divides Christmases forever after...when make-believe and sugar plum fairies and the chocolate milk and cookies left overnight suddenly become so many ghosts of holidays vanished.

Over the years, celebrations layered upon celebrations, weaving tapestries rich enough in experience to eclipse the year's frustrations. It took us a long time to learn that the most beautiful things in life take their hues from our own perspective and appreciation. And that memories are not the stories of where we have been, but the history of what we've become.

Looking back, Paw-Paw's long-ago walks serve as metaphors for the hills and mountains that we, our brothers and our cousins would all face in our lifetimes. We'd know many happy milestones, successes and triumphs. We'd also deal with crises, disappointments and tragedies, and the inevitable heartache of watching our parents grow old and die. Life never again offered us the sure-footed guidance and calm, steady presence of our grandfather, leading us back to Poplar Street in the late afternoons of our treasured remembrances.

Yet those walks enshrined a belief that lasted long past the festivities, the egg hunts and the decorations. We knew that we carried within us the compass of a family whose strengths endured in spite of the flaws that haunted it. When all else had fallen away, we emerged with a resilience more burnished than broken; it would see us through the challenges that taxed our energies, the storms that dashed our hopes.

If it is true that heritage means holding hands with forever, we count among our greatest blessings the hands that held ours.

They always pointed the way home.

*James Christopher Adler ("Paw-Paw"a.k.a. "Skinny
Jim Adler"), center, with his parents, John Gottlieb Adler
and Eliza Warnock Adler, probably circa 1900.*

*The family of Michael Reedy and Anna McKevitt Reedy, in what must
have been one of the family's few serious moments. Left to right, seated:
Michael Reedy, John Reedy ("Uncle Non"); Anna McKevitt Reedy;
Jeremiah Reedy ("Uncle Duddy"). Standing, left to right: Catherine
Reedy("Aunt Katie"); William Edward Reedy ("Uncle Bill"); Mary
Elizabeth Reedy ("Nana"); Francis Reedy ("Uncle Frank").*

Maizie Reedy, probably in her early 20s, about to "knock 'em dead."

Maizie Reedy with her younger brother, Frank Reedy. Frank, being in the Navy, was entitled to wear the uniform. Maizie was not.

*Louise Carpenter Adler and Justin Christopher Adler ("Uncle Dut
and Aunt Leeze") on their wedding day, December 27, 1939.*

Dorothea Adler Rowe ("Aunt Dokey") and William Marine Rowe ("Uncle Marine") on their wedding day, April 20, 1940. Paw-Paw is standing directly below the crucifix. Next to the officiating priest are John Adler ("Uncle Jack"), James Kevitt Adler ("Daddy"). At the far right, first row, is Justin Adler (" Uncle Dut"), standing next to Louise Carpenter Adler ("Aunt Leeze"). Justine Reedy ("Aunt Ding") the maid of honor, is to the immediate right of the bride.

A triumph of the Floating Blood Clot Novenas:
Daddy and Mother are married
on May 25, 1940. They are flanked by best man Justin
Adler ("Uncle Dut") on the left and by matron of honor Helen
Weber Wyninegar, Mother's beloved sister, on the right.

John W. Adler ("Uncle Jack") and Cassie Wilder Adler
("Aunt Cassie") on their 25th wedding anniversary.

Nana and Paw-Paw at the time of their golden wedding anniversary in 1956, a rare photo of the two of them side-by-side. "I'll tell you one thing," said Paw-Paw. "It was never dull."

Poplar Street's four Adler spawn, circa 1984. Left to right, Kevitt, Adrienne, Michele and Chris.

CPSIA information can be obtained at www.ICGtesting.com
Printed in the USA
LVOW131321260912

300421LV00005B/1/P

9 780976 674115